Football School

Name: ....

Class: ....

Coaches: ....

Kickito Ergo Sum

To Maya, midfield marvel — A.B.
To ABC, with love — B.L.

First published 2016 by Walker Books Ltd
87 Vauxhall Walk, London SE11 5HJ

2 4 6 8 10 9 7 5 3 1

This book has been typeset in Palatino

Printed and bound in Great Britain by Clays Ltd, St Ives plc

British Library Cataloguing in Publication Data:
a catalogue record for this book is available from the British Library

ISBN 978-1-4063-6724-9

WALKER
BOOKS

www.walker.co.uk

FOOTBALL SCHOOL

WHERE FOOTBALL ~~EXPLAINS~~ RULES THE WORLD

Alex Bellos & Ben Lyttleton

Welcome to Football School!
It's really great to meet you. I'm Alex.
And I'm Ben. We're your teachers.
But you can call us coaches - because this is not a normal school.
That's right! Every lesson here is about football.
The best kind of lesson! Because football is a great way to learn about the world.
You will learn stuff even your friends and parents don't know.
Like why geography makes Brazilians the most skilful players!
And how psychology can make you take the perfect penalty.
We'll give you a sniff of the biology of footballers' poo.
And show that sports photography is more than just clicking a button.
AB
BL
E=MC2

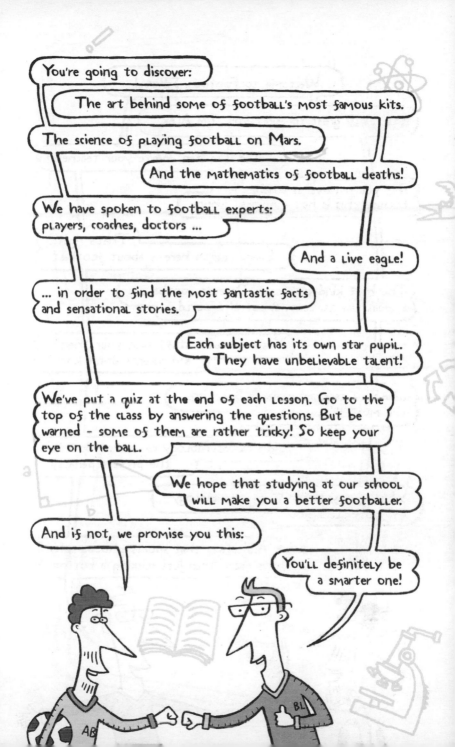

MEET YOUR COACHES

ALEX "BELLINHOS" BELLOS

66 Tudo bem, amigo? 99

COACH STATS

Birthplace: Oxford

Countries lived in: UK, Brazil

Home: London

Siblings: Two little sisters

First football memory: Scotland qualifying for the 1978 World Cup

Favourite football memory: Being in Rio de Janeiro when Brazil won the 2002 World Cup

Position: Right midfield

Real job: Writes books about maths, puzzles and Brazilian football

Dream job: Explorer

Supports: Paysandu Sport Club (Brazil)

Footballer pal: Pelé

Trick: Really good at calculating times tables. And league tables. And goal difference...

coach stats

Birthplace: London

Home: London

Siblings: One older brother

First football memory: Finishing my first Panini sticker album in 1981

Greatest football moment: Scoring a penalty in front of 25,000 fans

Favourite kit: Roma away, 2014–2015

Position: Left midfield

Real job: Football writer and pundit. Also a penalty expert

Dream job: Footballer

Supports: Littleton FC (Midland League Division One)

Footballer pal: Antonin Panenka

Trick: Never misses a penalty

BEN
"THE PEN"
LYTTLETON

66 Penalty, ref! 99

TIMETABLE

	MONDAY	TUESDAY
REGISTRATION		
LESSON 1	**BIOLOGY** 10–19	**ZOOLOGY** 42–53
LESSON 2	**ENGLISH** 20–31	**PHSE** 54–65
LESSON 3		**HISTORY** 66–77
LESSON 4	**MATHS** 32–41	
LUNCH		
LESSON 5	**MATHS**	**PSYCHOLOGY** 78–87

Are you as smart as our Star Pupils?

WEDNESDAY	THURSDAY	FRIDAY
8.30–8.40AM		
DESIGN TECHNOLOGY 88–97	**PHOTOGRAPHY** 132–143	**POLITICS** 174–185
	BUSINESS STUDIES 144–153	
GEOGRAPHY 98–109	**FASHION** 154–163	**MUSIC** 186–195
DRAMA 110–119		
1.00–2.00PM		
PHILOSOPHY 120–131	**COMPUTER SCIENCE** 164–173	**PHYSICS** 196–203

Find the answers to the quizzes on page 206. But no cheating!

BL

BIOLOGY

Welcome to the first lesson of the week at Football School. We're going to begin with the wonderful – and whiffy! – subject of poo.

Footballers take their digestive systems very seriously. Not only do they need to eat the right food so they stay fit and healthy, they also need to think about their poo. No one wants to be caught out in the middle of a game, as you can't rush to the toilet with 50,000 fans watching you. So top footballers plan when to go to the loo.

FARE PLAY

There are two parts to planning a poo. You need to eat the right sort of food, and you need to eat it at the right time. Footballers have special food doctors – called nutritionists – who make sure they eat properly. Here are two main meals often served before a match:

CHicken with boiled potatoes and carrots

FiSH with rice and broccoli

And here are two meals that would never be served before a match:

DouBLe cHeeseburger and extra CHiPs

Doughnuts

Food gives you the energy and the nutrients you need to survive. Potatoes and rice are served before matches because they contain lots of carbohydrates, which give you energy. Since you need lots of energy to run around for 90 minutes chasing a ball, footballers will have extra large helpings of potatoes and rice.

Footballers also eat lots of chicken and fish because they are packed with protein, which helps your body's cells grow and repair.

Vegetables like carrots and broccoli are a source of minerals and vitamins. These help boost your body's immune system that protects you from infection or illness.

Cheeseburgers, chips and doughnuts are full of fat. You don't want fat before a game because it causes the digestive system to slow down. The food sits in your stomach, making you feel full and heavy, which isn't good if you have to run around.

TOILET TIMINGS

In order to perfectly time a poo you need to plan when you eat. Clubs make sure their players eat a meal THREE HOURS before a game. This allows plenty of time for the food to pass through the digestive system.

The digestive system is the part of your body that takes in food, breaks it down, absorbs the nutrients and, last but not least, makes poo.

The journey starts with food entering the **mouth**. After you give it a good chew, the mashed-up food plummets down a long tube, called the **oesophagus**, to the **stomach**. There it is churned around and chemicals in the stomach break down the food, with the help of other organs such as the **liver** and **pancreas**. The final stage is the **small** and **large intestines**, where the nutrients are absorbed into the blood and what remains is expelled through

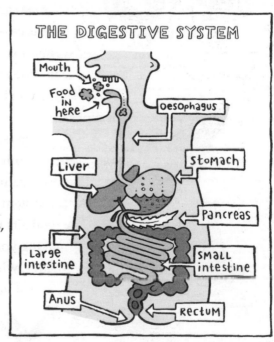

your **rectum** and **anus** (your bum) as poo. In an adult, the oesophagus, stomach and intestines – what we call our gut, or **alimentary canal** – is about nine metres long.

GET IT ALL OUT

By the time it's kick-off, a footballer's meal will have been completely broken down and any waste food will be ready to poo out. At one of the biggest clubs in the Premier League, there is a secret, malodorous ritual before a game starts. The players have a pooing procedure. They go to the toilet cubicles in a pre-determined order, partly based on seniority in the team. The most senior person poos first – for obvious, smell-related reasons! Then with empty stomachs they are ready for the game.

But it can be difficult to fix mealtimes (and pooing times) for footballers because kick-offs are spread throughout the day. Weekend kick-offs are at lunchtime or in the afternoon, and midweek kick-offs are in the evening.

Changing kick-offs are very disruptive to the players' digestive routine and a major cause of problems.

CLUB doctor

TUMMY TERROR

There's another reason why footballers tend to poo just before games, no matter what food they have eaten: fear.

When you get really, really scared, you want to poo. And just before a big match, a footballer will be full of fear. They will be scared of playing badly and losing.

Fear triggers funny feelings in our bellies because of an inbuilt survival system common to all animals. Imagine you are an animal minding your own business and all of a sudden another, bigger, nasty-looking animal appears in your path. You need to make an instant decision about whether to fight it or to run away. In either case – fight or flight – your muscles must be ready, so the body will start diverting blood to them.

Whenever humans sense danger and get scared, like a footballer before a game or a student before an exam, we respond in the same way. Blood is diverted to our muscles, we produce a chemical called adrenaline and the chemistry of our body is altered, making it feel extra sensitive. This also causes tension in our gut, which is what gives us that butterfly sensation, and can make us flee ... to the loo.

Remember, anyone can get butterflies in their stomachs even the most famous footballers in the world. And sometimes, despite all this pre-match planning, pooing can still go badly wrong.

The manager said it would be good to have some butterflies in my tummy.

HAVE WE GOT POOS FOR YOU

WIPE

Gary Lineker was one of England's best ever strikers. At the 1986 World Cup, he scored six goals and won the prize, known as the Golden Boot, for top scorer. But the 1990 World Cup started quite, well, poo-rly for him. "I tried to tackle someone, stretched and relaxed myself and erm..." Lineker said of the moment he pooed himself on the pitch against the Republic of Ireland in England's first game of the tournament. "I was not very well, I was poorly at half-time. I was very fortunate that it rained that night so I could do something about it, but it was messy. You can see myself rubbing the ground like a dog trying to clean it. It was the most horrendous experience of my life." There was some good news: the Irish players did not want to get too close to him. "I have never found so much space after that in my life," he laughed.

FOUL

Mexico were drawing 1–1 with local rivals the USA in 2011 and there were just a few minutes left to play when Mexican midfielder Omar Arellano bent down to adjust his socks. As the TV cameras panned in for a close-up, there was a surprise for viewers: a suspicious-looking

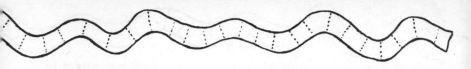

brown stain on the back of his white shorts, which was aired around the world.

YUK

"I was on two lots of antibiotics at the time for a kick on my leg, which resulted in an upset stomach," said Welsh midfielder Robbie Savage about the day his Leicester City team played Aston Villa in the Premier League in April 2002. "I had a bad case of diarrhoea on the day of the game, so had to go there and then, and the nearest place was the referee's toilet." It was an expensive decision: the referee, Graham Poll, reported him to the Football Association for "improper conduct" and Savage had to pay a £10,000 fine.

CHEEK

English winger Jason Puncheon ran off the pitch in the middle of the second half during a Premier League game for Southampton against Everton in 2013. He returned a few minutes later with a grin on his face and the fans chanting a song that suggested he had gone for a poo. Puncheon appeared to confirm their suspicions when he celebrated scoring his next goal a couple of weeks later: he ran to the corner flag, bent down and pretended to wipe his bum.

DOGGIE DOO

Football is not the only sport where poo is better out than in. In greyhound racing, it is said that the dog who does a poo just before the start will win the race. Fans like to keep a close eye on the dogs just in case any of them start to squat…

No privacy these days.

☆ STAR PUPIL

TOMMY ACHE

★ ★ ★ ★

66 It wasn't me! 99

☆☆☆ STAR PUPIL Stats

Favourite number: 2
Daily intake of prunes: 25
Butterflies in stomach: 324
Pants worn under shorts: 3
Birthplace: Crapstone, England
Supports: Arsenal (UK)
Fave player: Kaka
Trick: Smelling danger

☆

BIOLOGY QUIZ

1. Which of the following is NOT part of the digestive system?

a) Oesophagus
b) Stomach
c) Liver
d) Nose

2. If an adult stretched out his or her intestines they would be as long as:

a) the height of a goal post.
b) the width of a goal.
c) the width of a football pitch.
d) the distance from the centre circle to the nearest toilet.

3. How many times will a person fart on average every 100 minutes?

a) 0 times
b) 1 time
c) 10 times
d) 100 times

4. What was Brazilian striker Ronaldo caught doing while playing in a match at the 1996 Olympic Games?

a) Eating his bogey
b) Farting in an opponent's face
c) Weeing out of the side of his shorts
d) Burping at the referee

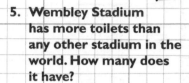

5. Wembley Stadium has more toilets than any other stadium in the world. How many does it have?

a) 418
b) 818
c) 1,318
d) 2,618

ENGLISH

This lesson is about the language of football. In order to enjoy the game, you need to be able to talk the talk. Can you tell the difference between a howler and a screamer? No, it's not about the noise they make.

Football language is famous for its **clichés**, which are expressions that are used so much they become completely unoriginal things to say. An example is "it's a funny old game". You may have spotted a few in our cartoon.

Today we are looking at the *ABCD*, which is short for *Alex and Ben's Classroom Dictionary*. It is full of football **jargon**, which is the special language that is not understood by outsiders. We explain some of the intriguing origins of these words and phrases. The vocabulary will help you understand the game at a deeper level. It will also mean that when you listen to commentators or professional players, you will be able to understand the words they are using – even if they are talking nonsense, which they often are!

Alex and Ben's Classroom Dictionary

4-4-2 • a tactical formation that refers to four defenders, four midfielders and two attacking players in the starting eleven. Goalkeepers are not mentioned as everyone knows they are there. 4-4-2 has traditionally been the most common formation in English football, although today's teams often play with four defenders, two defensive midfielders, three attacking midfielders and one centre-forward. This formation is called a 4-2-3-1. ☻

the beautiful game • a phrase often used to describe football. It's an English translation of the Portuguese phrase "o jogo bonito", which was made famous by Alex's mate, the Brazilian footballer Pelé. ○ ☺

bicycle kick • a kick where the player jumps and swings one foot to kick the ball over their head while their body is horizontal. At the moment of the kick it looks like the player is riding an imaginary bicycle in the air. The bicycle kick is not to be confused with the overhead kick, which is when the player hangs vertically upside down to kick the ball. ☛

Key players

➤ Famous bicycle kicks

Mark Hughes
(**Wales** v. Spain, 1985)
Jean-Pierre Papin
(**France** v. Belgium, 1992)
Peter Crouch
(**Liverpool** v. Galatasaray, 2006)
Wayne Rooney
(**Manchester United** v. Manchester City, 2011)
Lisa De Vanna
(**Sky Blue** v. Boston Breakers, 2013)

Key | ☻ = tactic | ☺ = origin | ☛ = technique | ○ = jargon

bogey team • "Bogey" is an old word for a ghost, goblin or evil spirit. A bogey team is one you always lose to, or who bring you bad luck. In golf the word is also linked to bad luck: a bogey is a score of one more than the expected score, or par, for a hole. In neither case are bogeys related to the green stuff that comes out your nose. ○

brace • when two goals are scored by the same player in the same match, it is called a brace. This comes from the French word for arms ("bras"), of which we have two. ○ ♀

catenaccio • a system of defensive play invented in Italy that uses an extra player behind the defence to ensure all attacks on the goal are blocked. When the strategy works, the attacking side cannot get through. "Catenaccio" is Italian for "doorbolt". ☺ ♀

(El) Clásico • most commonly used to mean a match between Spanish clubs Real Madrid and Barcelona. It can also mean any match between two rival teams, usually from the same area, in Spanish-speaking countries such as Argentina or Mexico. ♀ ○

clean sheet • when a team doesn't let in any goals in a match. In America, this is known as a shutout. ○

derby *(pronounced "darby")* • a match between two teams from the same area. The word comes from the 12th Earl of Derby, who founded a famous horse race in 1780 at Epsom, near London, which is still held

Alex and Ben's Classroom Dictionary

every year. The term "derby" came to be used for any grand sporting event, and then for an important sporting event between two local teams. �

drubbing • a resounding defeat, such as the game in 2002 when Stade Olympique L'Emyrne, the previous season's champions of Madagascar, lost 149–0 to rivals AS Adema. The match holds the world record for the highest score in professional football. Even though SOE lost the game, they scored all 149 goals. This is because they were all own goals scored in protest at refereeing decisions that had gone against them in previous matches. The SOE coach was banned from football for three years after the game. ◯

Stats and facts

➤ Famous derbies

COUNTRY	RIVAL TEAMS	NAME OF DERBY
England	Manchester United v. Liverpool	North-West Derby
France	Paris Saint-Germain v. Marseille	Le Classique
Germany	Borussia Dortmund v. Bayern Munich	Der Klassiker
Italy	Inter Milan v. Juventus	Derby d'Italia
Portugal	Benfica v. Porto	O Classico
Spain	Real Madrid v. Barcelona	El Clásico

➤ Famous drubbings

YEAR	COUNTRY	WINNERS	LOSERS	SCORE
1885	Scotland	Arbroath	Bon Accord	36–0
1971	Tahiti	Tahiti	Cook Islands	30–0
2001	Australia	Australia	American Samoa	31–0
2013	Nigeria	Plateau United Feeders	Akurba	79–0

Key | 🌐 = tactic | 🌱 = origin | ✊ = technique | ◯ = jargon

dugout • the bench or benches where the coach and substitutes sit during a match. It used to be dug out of the ground but usually isn't any more. ○

fair-weather fan • a fan who supports their team only when the team are doing well. The comparison is to a person who goes outside in good weather, but stays indoors when the weather is bad. So a fair-weather fan stops supporting a team when they are losing. ○

galáctico *("galactic" in Spanish)* • originally a name for the star players recruited by Real Madrid, this is now used to describe only the most famous international players. The term comes from a description of football as coming from another galaxy. ⊛

group of death • a group in the first stages of a competition with so many strong teams that at least one of them will be knocked out early. ○

Alex and Ben's Classroom Dictionary

hat-trick • when three goals are scored by the same player in the same match. The term dates back to 1858, when the cricketer H. H. Stephenson took three wickets with three consecutive deliveries. Fans were so impressed they raised some money and bought him a hat. The phrase "hat-trick" caught on and became used in other sports. The perfect hat-trick in football consists of one goal scored with the left foot, one with the right foot and one with the head. ○ ℗

magic sponge • used by club doctors to treat players when they are lying on the pitch injured. It's just a normal sponge with no real magic powers, but often a splash of cold water can help hurt players recover. Cold water reduces the blood supply to the injured area, preventing swelling and allowing the players to get back to the game. That's why the sponge is seen as magical. ○

Matildas • the nickname for the Australia national women's team, after "Waltzing Matilda", the most famous song in Australia and the country's unofficial national anthem. ○ ℗

nutmeg • to nutmeg means to pass the ball through an

Key | ⊕ = tactic | ℗ = origin | 👋 = technique | ○ = jargon

opponent's legs. The origin of the verb is not known, although several derivations have been suggested: **1.** The word nutmeg is Cockney rhyming slang for leg. **2.** The nutmeg is a reference to the "nuts", or testicles, of

the player between whose legs the ball is passed. **3.** In the nineteenth century the phrase "to be nutmegged" meant "to be deceived", since nutmegs were very expensive and often sellers conned people by adding wooden nuts into bags of nutmegs.

parking the bus • when almost all of the players in a team stay in defence. This has the same effect as parking the team bus in front of their goal.

➤ Anyone for nutmeg?

Other countries have their own unique words and phrases to describe the act of kicking a ball between a player's legs.

LANGUAGE	TERM
Arabic (Egypt, Jordan, Syria)	egg
Austrian	gherkin
Danish	tunnel
Dutch	gate
Finnish	collar
French	little bridge
German	tunnel
Hebrew	to thread a needle
Italian	tunnel
Korean	to hatch an egg
Portuguese (Brazil)	pen
Spanish (Latin America)	spout
Swedish	tunnel
Turkish	cradle

plum tie • not a cravat with a purple fruit pattern on it, but a particularly exciting fixture. Plum can also mean "desirable", and the word tie means a sports event.

poacher • in football, a poacher is a striker who loiters around the goal area and is particularly lethal at scoring from fleeting chances. The name is because a poacher is someone who goes hunting in places they are not allowed to. 🌝 🗨

rabona • a "crossed" kick in which the kicking foot goes round the back of the standing leg, thus making the legs cross. In 1948 the Argentinian player Ricardo Infante scored the earliest recorded goal like this – from 35 yards out. When reporting on the match, a local sports magazine wanted to get across the cheekiness of the move, so it said that Infante – whose name means "child" in Spanish – was doing a "rabona", meaning he was skipping school. The name stuck. 🎙 🖐

six-pointer • a game between two teams who are neck-and-neck in the league table, usually towards the end of the season and when the teams are in the running for promotion or relegation. The winners of a game of football get three points, and the losers get no points. When the teams are neck-and-neck, however, not only do the winners get three points, but the losers are also denied the three points that they could have got had they been playing another team. The three points gained plus the three points denied adds up to six points. 🗨

Key players

➤ Rabona experts

Eden Hazard
Erik Lamela
Angel di Maria
Neymar
Cristiano Ronaldo

Key | 🌝 = tactic | 🎙 = origin | 🖐 = technique | 🗨 = jargon

square ball • when a ball is passed sideways, rather than forwards or backwards. Not a ball that isn't round.

stepover • a trick where the player moves their foot over the ball without touching it, so as to fool the opposing player into thinking that they are moving with the ball in that direction. Pedro Calomino, an Argentinian player for Boca Juniors in the early twentieth century, is believed to have invented it.

supersub • a substitute who often wins games by scoring a crucial late goal. Some strikers are experts at coming on to the pitch and finding space when defenders are tired.

tiki-taka • a style of football, developed at Barcelona, where the players make lots of short passes and maintain possession for long periods.

vuvuzela • a plastic horn that makes a very loud noise when you blow it, and which was used by fans at the 2010 World Cup in South Africa.

Key players

> **Supersub kings**

Roger Milla (Cameroon, 1973–94)
David Fairclough (Liverpool, 1975–83)
Ole Gunnar Solskjaer (Manchester United, 1996–2007)
Henrik Larsson (Barcelona, 2004–06)
Mohamed Nagy (Egypt, 2009–)

KICK-TIONARY CORNER

The nine words below can be used for different types of kick, from a terrible one (howler) to a brilliant one (screamer). Can you think of any others?

HUMDINGER ROCKET
BLINDER PILEDRIVER
STINKER STUNNER
SHOCKER SCREAMER
HOWLER

The Kickometer

DICK SHUNRIE

☆ STAR PUPIL

Football theory

66 What do you mean! 99

☆☆☆ STAR PUPIL Stats

Vocabulary: 50,000 words
Reading speed: 1 page per minute
Scrabble score: $D_2I_1C_3K_5$
$S_1H_4U_1N_1R_1I_1E_1 = 21$
Syllables: 3
Birthplace: Verbier, Switzerland
Supports: ABC (Brazil)
Fave player: Anthony Wordsworth
Trick: Doesn't need spellcheck

ENGLISH QUIZ

1. Which of the following clichés is NOT used for scoring a goal?

a) Finding the back of the net
b) Beating the keeper
c) Rattling the woodwork
d) Slamming it home

2. Which is the correct cliché? The striker leapt like a:

a) Giraffe
b) Kangaroo
c) Flea
d) Salmon

3. What is a banana kick?

a) A goal scored by a player in yellow boots
b) A pass or shot that curls
c) A goalkeeper's kick that goes so high monkeys in trees could catch it
d) When a player slips on the pitch

4. What is a Christmas tree formation?

a) A tradition in Lapland where the league leader at Christmas gives presents to opposition fans
b) A pile of dirty boots that look like presents at the bottom of a tree
c) A tactical system of 4-3-2-1, which when viewed from above has the shape of a Christmas tree
d) The league table on 25 December

5. Why is the ripple effect that goes around a stadium when fans stand up with their hands in the air and then sit down again called a "Mexican wave"?

a) Mexico's coast has the highest waves in the world
b) A Mexican fan once threw a fajita up in the air because it burnt his mouth and others copied him
c) They became popular during the 1986 World Cup in Mexico
d) Mexico City has lots of roundabouts

MATHS

G et your calculators out! This lesson we're doing some sums.

We're going to work out the risk of dying during a game of football – because some really unlucky things could happen to you on the pitch.

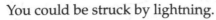

You could be struck by lightning.

You could be whacked by a falling crossbar.

You could collide with a wall by the side of the pitch.

You could score a goal, celebrate by somersaulting in the air, land badly and break your back.

Footballers have died in all these circumstances. :-(
We don't want any of you to die at Football School, so we're going to find out how dangerous football really is. We'll also discover what is the greatest health risk to footballers and what's being done about it.

But just to be safe: don't play during lightning storms, check the crossbar, don't run into walls and practise your somersaults.

WHAT ARE THE CHANCES?

In order to calculate the risk of dying while playing football, we need to count all the people who have died playing football and divide this number by the total number of people who have ever played football.

Because this is maths, we can write this as an **equation**:

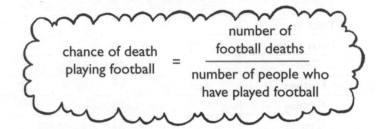

$$\text{chance of death playing football} = \frac{\text{number of football deaths}}{\text{number of people who have played football}}$$

Easy! Well, not quite. It is impossible to know all the people who have ever died playing football, since no one has kept a list.

However, a university in Germany counted all the people in one city who died playing sports over a ten-year period. We are going to use this data to calculate the annual risk of a person dying during a game of football.

The table below shows the number of deaths from different sports in Hamburg, a city with a population of 1.7 million, between 1997 and 2006. Table tennis had the fewest deaths, swimming the most, and football is in the middle.

SPORT	NUMBER OF DEATHS BETWEEN 1997-2006 INCLUSIVE
Table tennis	7
Horse riding	10
Tennis	15
Football	17
Running	18
Cycling	19
Swimming	31

In order to calculate the chances of dying while playing football in Hamburg we need to divide 17 – the number of football deaths – by the total number of people in Hamburg who played football in that ten year period.

But how do we find out how many Hamburgers play football? According to FIFA, one fifth of the total population of Germany plays football. We can therefore assume that one fifth of the population of Hamburg played football during that time. That's one fifth of 1.7 million, which is:

$$1,700,000 \div 5 = 340,000$$

Now we can return to the equation and do our calculation.

In Hamburg for the period between 1997 and 2006 inclusive, we can say that:

$$\text{chance of death playing football} = \frac{\text{number of football deaths}}{\text{number of people who have played football}} = \frac{17}{340,000}$$

When we divide top and bottom by 17 we get:

$$= \frac{1}{20,000} \quad \text{or 1 in 20,000}$$

So, in the ten years from 1997 to 2006, one person in 20,000 died in Hamburg playing football. We want to find the chance of dying in a single year, which is going to be one-tenth the chance of dying over ten years. One tenth of 1/20,000 is 1/10 x 1/20,000 = 1/200,000, or 1 in 200,000.

We have our answer! We've calculated that between 1997 and 2006, the annual chance of dying while playing a game of football in Hamburg was about 1 in 200,000.

We can assume that the number has stayed about the same, because it wasn't long ago. And since the lifestyle in Hamburg is similar to the UK, we can generalize and say that the annual chance of death playing football in the UK is probably also about 1 in 200,000.

But that's not *your* chance of dying while playing football. The 1 in 200,000 figure applies to all people: young and old, professional and amateur, fat and thin. The Hamburg study found that most football deaths were from heart attacks. Those most at risk were unfit adults, whose hearts were not able to take the pressure of vigorous exercise. If you are young and healthy, the risk of dying from a heart attack while playing football is very, very small.

And the risk of being hit by a lightning strike or a crossbar falling on your head is even smaller.

BROKEN HEART

In rare cases, top footballers have suffered from a weak heart. In 2003, midfielder Marc-Vivien Foé collapsed and died while playing for Cameroon against Colombia in the Confederations Cup semi-final. It turned out that Foé had a type of heart disease that had gone undetected all his life.

As a result of Foé's death, FIFA introduced safety procedures to try to make sure no professional died from an undetected heart condition ever again. In the top leagues players are now screened for heart disease before tournaments. Major stadiums must have **defibrillators**, which are machines used on people who have had heart attacks. They deliver electric shocks through the chest that can return the heart to a normal rhythm.

These new procedures have already saved a life.

In 2012 Bolton Wanderers midfielder Fabrice Muamba was playing an FA Cup match against Tottenham Hotspur. After 43 minutes, he suddenly fell to the ground. His heart had stopped beating. This is called a **cardiac arrest** and happens when the heart stops pumping blood around the body. He was 23 years old.

Medical staff hurried to help Muamba and gave him **cardio pulmonary resuscitation**, known as CPR, pumping the chest to artificially keep oxygen flowing around the body. The team also used the stadium's defibrillators.

Muamba's heart did not beat for 78 minutes before it started working properly again. One Spurs fan who was at the game, Dr Andrew Deaner, rushed onto the pitch to help and then treated Muamba at the London Chest Hospital, where he worked. Muamba thanked Deaner and everyone was happy at the result – even the Spurs fans.

LET'S HAVE SUM FUN

There are safer ways of talking about maths at Football School. Alex developed his love of numbers when he was at school by looking at league tables and working out the goal difference between teams.

$2+2+2$

That was taken one step further in Romania, when the national team had fun with their shirt numbers for a friendly against Spain. The players wore sums on their backs, and the answer to the sum was their normal shirt number.

2×7

The player who usually wore 6 wore $2 + 2 + 2$. The player who wore $46 \div 2$ had squad number 23, and the number 14 was now 2×7. The head of Romanian football, Ben's friend Razvan Burleanu, said they did it to give children a different way of discovering maths. Razvan has the right idea: he can come and teach maths at Football School anytime.

$\frac{46}{2}$

5^2

IVAN A LAUGH

Chilean striker Iván Zamorano took a leaf out of Romania's maths book back in 1998 when he lost his favourite shirt number to Brazilian teammate Ronaldo at Inter Milan. Ronaldo was given the number 9 shirt but Zamorano wanted to keep his number, so he wore 18 but made the kit designers add a little + sign between the numbers – as 1 + 8 = 9. Good thinking Iván!

LUCKY S. CAPES

STAR PUPIL

" Take the risk! "

STAR PUPIL Stats

Broken bones: 24
Hospital visits: 312
Annual spend on plasters: €2,500
Favourite number: 999
Birthplace: Providence, USA
Supports: San Jose Earthquakes (USA)
Fave player: Luis Boa Morte
(surname is Portuguese for "good death")
Trick: Parachutes onto pitch

MATHS QUIZ

1. Which sport causes the most deaths according to research mentioned in the lesson?

a) Swimming
b) Running
c) Horse riding
d) Table tennis

2. If the chances of something happening are 4 in 20, this is the same as:

a) 1 in 3
b) 1 in 4
c) 1 in 5
d) 1 in 20

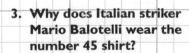

3. Why does Italian striker Mario Balotelli wear the number 45 shirt?

a) He changes his hairstyle 45 times a year.
b) He scored 45 goals in his first season as a professional.
c) He wanted to wear number 9 and $4 + 5 = 9$.
d) He was born in 1945.

4. What shirt number was Moroccan striker Hicham Zerouali allowed to wear when he played for Scottish club Aberdeen in 2000?

a) 0
b) 1
c) 1000
d) Infinity

5. What did the referee do when Croatian defender Goran Tunjic collapsed after a heart attack in a fifth division game in 2010?

a) He gave him mouth-to-mouth resuscitation.
b) He booked him for diving.
c) He asked if there were any doctors in the crowd.
d) He carried him off the pitch and waved play on.

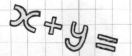

Tuesday
Lesson 1

ZOOLOGY

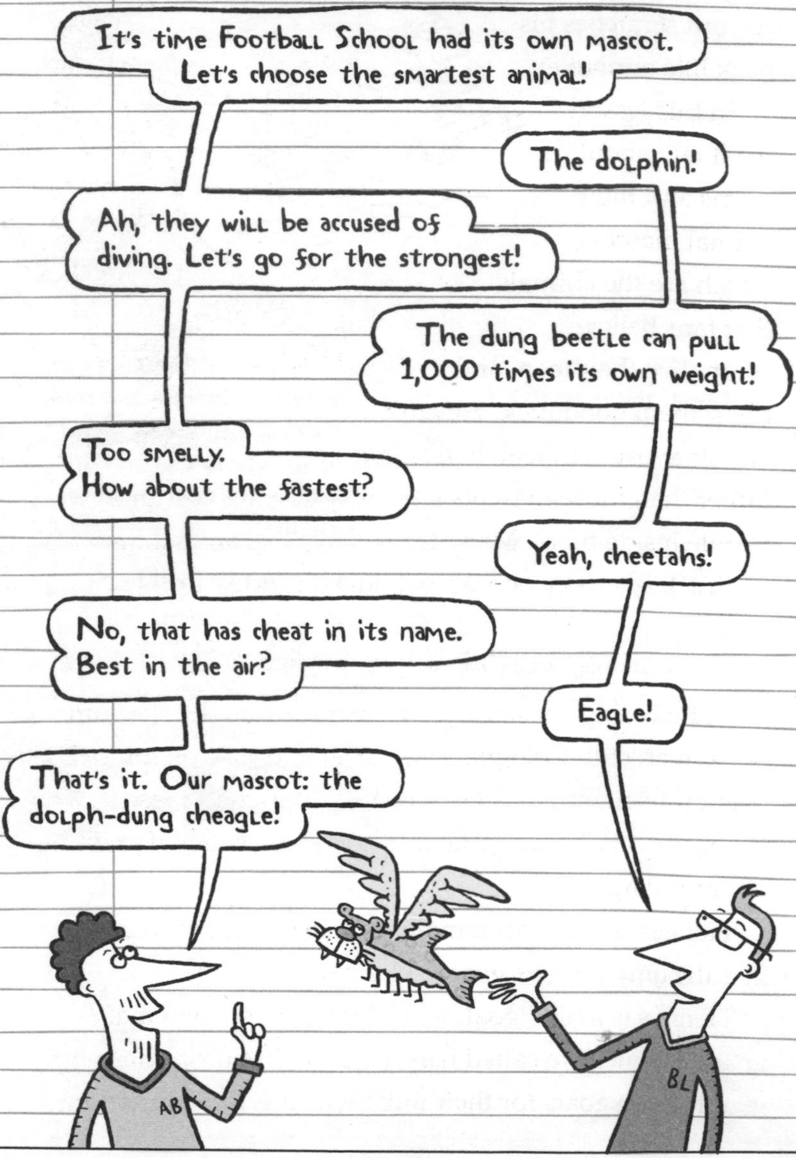

Enough about death! Here at Football School we prefer life in all its manifestations – especially animals. Ben has a pet dog who he runs with every day in the park.

Alex doesn't have a pet but scratches his back like a monkey.

In this lesson we'll talk about teams and their animal mascots, which are the animals that fans believe symbolize their team and bring them good luck. We are only interested in real, live animals, rather than those mascots who are just giant costumes with people inside them. Many teams have live animal mascots. Their job is a risky one, as we will see. Giddy up!

GOOOAAAAAAAAT

A goat wearing a snazzy red cloak trots into the stadium of German club Cologne. Fans cheer and take pictures. The glamorous mammal is Hennes VIII, Cologne's mascot, who watches every home game from the same patch of grass by a corner flag.

Hennes is the most famous goat in Germany. In fact, he's the only famous goat in Germany!

Hennes is a billy goat, which is the name for a male goat. (Females are called nanny goats.) In Europe, farmers mainly keep goats for their milk, which is then turned into cheese. But in Africa, Asia and the Caribbean, goat meat is a speciality – don't tell Hennes!

During matches Hennes stands next to his handler Ingo Reipka, who keeps him on a short leather leash. The goat munches on carrots and bread and even finds the pitch tasty. "Sometimes he eats the grass – the only thing he doesn't like is the white markings," says Reipka. Hennes gets a bit restless when the linesman runs past him, and he isn't so keen when the action comes his way because he is afraid of the ball.

On one occasion Nigerian striker Anthony Ujah got in trouble over Hennes. After scoring a goal for Cologne, he ran to where Hennes was standing and pulled his horns. Ouch! Reipka had to calm the billy goat down. Ujah later said, "Apologies to Hennes for my hard celebration."

The goat is called Hennes VIII because he is the eighth goat called Hennes to occupy the role of Cologne mascot. It is said that the tradition started in 1950, when a circus owner gave a billy goat to the club as a lucky charm. They named him after Hennes Weisweiler, who was Cologne coach at the time.

Goats only have a lifespan of about fifteen years, so when Hennes died he was replaced by Hennes II, and so on until Hennes VIII became the mascot in 2008 after an online ballot of fans to choose between four candidates. The most famous of Cologne's goats was Hennes VII. He even appeared in TV shows, including once as a murder victim in a German crime drama. Hennes used to travel with the players on the team coach, but it's safer for his handler to take him to games on his own. Hennes VIII now lives in a log cabin in Cologne Zoo which he shares with Anneliese, his favourite nanny goat. The cabin has a fireplace filled with hay, and the walls are covered with Cologne flags and photos.

The Hennes tradition became so popular with the club that he is now on their club badge, and Cologne are known in Germany as the Billy Goats.

A legendary goatherd from Ethiopia called Kaldi is said to have discovered the coffee plant when he saw his goats dancing after they nibbled the plant's berries.

Scientists say that some goats' accents change to fit their surroundings when they move away from their family.

Cashmere is a super-soft wool produced by cashmere goats. It got its name as it was first made in a region in South Asia called Kashmir.

goat facts

- 45 -

YOU HAVE GOAT TO BE KIDDING ME

Cologne are not the only football team with a horned history. Over 100 years ago, Manchester United had a goat as a mascot. In 1906 the director of Benson's, a travelling theatre company, gave defender Charlie Roberts a goat called Billy. No one knows why. A dog called Major had been United's mascot, but Billy took over the duties. Before every match, he was paraded around the pitch. After some games, Billy even went with the players to the local pub and toasted wins with a little drink.

Billy's last game was the 1909 FA Cup final, when Manchester United beat Bristol City 1–0. He joined the Manchester United players celebrating after the game, but he died of suspected alcohol poisoning soon after. It was thought that he had drunk too much beer or champagne. That was the last time Manchester United had a live animal as a mascot. *Hic!*

OWL ABOUT THAT?

As Billy proved, being a mascot can be a dangerous job. In 2011 a Colombian league game turned ugly after Panamanian defender Luis Moreno was accused by opposition fans of "murdering" an owl during a match. The owl, who lived in the stadium roof, was the mascot of the Barranquilla side Atlético Junior. He had been hit

by the ball and was lying on the pitch with an injured leg. Moreno, apparently keen for the game to continue, was seen to kick the owl towards the touchline with his left foot. Fans chanted "Murderer!" at the player. Vets were later unable to save the owl's life. Moreno apologized "to the entire Colombian country" and was given a lecture about owls at his local zoo. He promised to return to the zoo once a month to help out.

Lots of owl species have asymmetrical ears that are different sizes and different heights on their heads.

Owls have three eyelids: one for blinking, one for sleeping and one for keeping the eye clean and healthy.

All owls hoot, but some make other noises too. The barn owl hisses when it is scared.

EAGLES HAVE LANDED

Talking of birds, did you know the most common animal mascot for football teams is the eagle?

The eagle, in fact, has been a symbol of strength, superiority and courage since ancient times, because of its awesome fighting skills and beautiful appearance.

Eagles are birds of prey, which means that they kill and eat other animals. Usually they go for small mammals like rabbits and mice, but they can even kill wolves and foxes.

Eagles are speedy birds. They can fly at up to 55 mph and can dive at 100 mph, which is faster than cars on the motorway.

Their eyesight is incredible too. We have eyes on the front of our face and so can only see forwards, but eagles have eyes on the sides of their head so they can see forwards, to the sides and (almost) behind themselves. On top of this, their eyesight is around four times better than ours. They can spot a rabbit from a mile away. That's why when someone is very observant we call them "eagle-eyed".

One expert told us that the eagle's beaked face makes it look majestic. No wonder that throughout history the eagle has been called the "king of the skies".

SPQR
FC

This team is of a high standard!

REGAL EAGLES

In ancient Rome the eagle represented power, freedom, wisdom and nobility. Every unit of soldiers in an ancient Roman army had an eagle **standard**, which was the military equivalent of a mascot. Losing the eagle standard would represent defeat for the army.

Eagle

Top of the food chain

Haughty, noble expression

Rules the countryside

Luxurious mantle

Powerful claws

Fearless predator

King

Top of the monarchy

Haughty, noble expression

Rules the country

Luxurious mantle

Powerful sword

Fearless leader

This is why the Italian team Lazio, who are based in Rome, have an eagle on their badge and fly a live eagle, called Olimpia, around the stadium before games. "The eagle is very important for us, it is our history," explained Lazio owner Claudio Lotito. Olimpia lives at the club training ground and receives regular visits from Lazio fans and players.

Ancient Rome's use of the eagle as a symbol of freedom spread around the world. In 1782 the USA adopted the bald eagle, which can only be found in North America, as its national bird. Today some Native Americans use eagle feathers on headdresses as they believe they have religious and spiritual significance.

In 1904 the Portuguese team Sport Lisboa, who later became Benfica, were one of the first teams to use the eagle as a sports emblem. Other teams followed suit. In 1973 Crystal Palace's manager Malcolm Allison changed the club's nickname from The Glaziers to The Eagles – because Benfica was one of Europe's top teams at the time.
Now lots of teams are known as The Eagles.

KAYLA THE EAGLE

Crystal Palace's nickname stuck and the eagle was adopted as the club's mascot. In captivity, eagles can live until they are 50. Kayla, the current Crystal Palace mascot, is in her mid-twenties, so has many more years of flying around the stadium before games and at half-time. Kayla was born in Canada, but in 2010 she moved to England and became the London team's mascot.

We will stop at nothing to find out fascinating facts for you, so we spoke to her handler, Alan Ames. He said that her full wingspan of 2 metres is a very impressive sight, but you need to keep an eye on her: sometimes she will leave a poo-shaped present on opposition fans' heads. He told us that when Millwall fans chanted, "You're just a pigeon!" at her, she swooped down but was not quite able to snatch one fan's pork pie.

Ames says that crowds never stress Kayla out but a strong wind does. Before one match, a powerful gust blew her above the roof of the stadium and she was temporarily lost. Luckily she was wearing a tracking device and her handler quickly found her.

She loves meeting fans although she is not sure what to make of Palace's other eagle mascots, Pete and Alice, who are adults wearing eagle costumes. "She thinks they are prats in fancy dress and she mostly ignores them," said Ames. "She knows that she's the boss."

KAYLA SPEAKS

We even interviewed the most famous eagle in football.
(We had to use her handler Alan Ames as our interpreter as
he told us he speaks Eaglish.)

Favourite player?

The goalkeeper; he didn't drop me.

Favourite band?

Kings of Leon. I was on their album cover.

What do you think of humans?

Crazy, I only work for 8 minutes a day.

Favourite song?

Eagles! Eagles!

ROBYN BIRD

☆ STAR PUPIL

66 I'm on the wing! 99

☆☆☆ STAR PUPIL | Stats

Pets: 286
Number of legs on pets: 1,427
(includes Sammy the 7-legged spider)
Arm span: 5 feet
Highest whistle frequency: 46 kHz
Birthplace: Cowes, England
Supports: Wolfsburg (Germany)
Favourite player: Chris Eagles
Trick: Predator in the box
☆

ZOOLOGY QUIZ

1. Which of the following is a bird of prey?

a) Chicken
b) Flamingo
c) Eagle
d) Robin

2. What animal are all dogs descended from?

a) Wolf
b) Hairy mammoth
c) Rabbit
d) Fox

3. Three of these countries have an eagle on their national flags. The fourth has another kind of winged animal. Which country is it, and what's the animal?

a) Albania
b) Mexico
c) Wales
d) Egypt

4. What is the name of the Canadian Club Toronto's flying mascot?

a) Bitchy the Hawk
b) Freddy the Falcon
c) Ticker the Rooster
d) Stolly the Unicorn

5. Which team is nicknamed the Monkey Hangers after people in their town hanged a monkey in the early 1800s because they thought it was a French spy?

a) Scunthorpe United
b) Hartlepool United
c) Crewe Alexandra
d) Plymouth Argyle

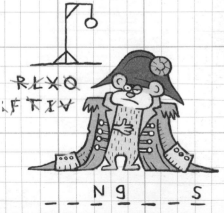

RLXQ
IFTIV

_ _ _ N g _ _ _ S

PHSE

re you an only child? Do you have brothers or sisters? If so, are you the eldest, youngest or in the middle?

And what on earth does this have to do with football? Quite a lot, actually.

This lesson is about the influence of our families on our football skills. Mum and Dad play a role, obviously – but so do brothers and sisters. It turns out that your chances of footballing glory are influenced by whether you were born first or last.

One final question: when is your birthday? This is also important to your footballing career. (And we want to send you a birthday card.)

SIBLING SUCCESS

Brothers and sisters can be really, really annoying. But here's the rub: if you want to be a professional footballer, they can be really useful to have.

This is because chances are your siblings are often around at home. When you want to kick a ball around, they will be there to play with as ready-made teammates. And the more you practise, the better you will be.

Take the case of Paul Pogba, the French midfielder, and his twin older brothers, Florentin and Mathias. "I told Paul he was wasting his time playing with kids his own age, so he played with me and Mathias," said Florentin, who is two years older. "It was hard for him but it built up his character. Sometimes he came home in tears because we were stronger than him, but it helped him improve."

Mathias added, "Paul, as the youngest, wanted to be like us... We told him: 'Come and play with us and your game will progress quicker, you'll become stronger.' Just look at him now. It worked." Eventually, Paul became better than his brothers and one of the French team's most important players. Florentin and Mathias play for Guinea, the African country where their dad was born.

LITTLE TERRORS

As in the case of Paul Pogba, it is often really helpful to have siblings who are older than you, since you will be forced to play at their level. Some of the world's best strikers have older brothers or sisters.

PLAYER	OLDER SIBLINGS
Gareth Bale (Wales)	Vicky
Harry Kane (England)	Charlie
Marta (Brazil)	Angela, Valdir and José
Lionel Messi (Argentina)	Rodrigo and Matias
Luis Suarez (Uruguay)	Paolo, Giovanna and Leticia

Scientists have investigated the phenomenon of younger siblings doing better than older siblings in sport. Dr Michael Perkin, an expert in child health at St George's Hospital in London, counted the number of eldest, middle and youngest children among footballers in one league in English football. He discovered that 46 per cent – that's almost half – of the footballers surveyed were youngest children.

It really is an advantage being the baby in the family!

Only children 4%

Eldest children 28%

Youngest children 46%

Middle children 22%

Research into other sports has shown that youngest children play in a different way from eldest children. For example, a study found elder children who play baseball feel more responsibility and don't take many risks, while youngest children take more risky decisions during play.

Taking risks isn't good if you are a goalkeeper, but it can be a really useful thing if you are further up the field. Sometimes risks can lead to scoring great goals.

Dr Perkin made another discovery. He showed that the average number of siblings a player has changes depending on their position.

On average, if you only have one sibling, you're more likely to be in goal. And on the whole, attackers have more brothers and sisters than defenders.

Goalkeepers
1.1 siblings

Defenders
1.8 siblings

Strikers
2.0 siblings

Midfielders
2.4 siblings

Although this doesn't always hold true. Former France captain Patrice Evra has 24 (yes, TWENTY-FOUR) brothers and sisters. And yet he was a defender. Imagine trying to brush your teeth in the morning in a house that size...

FULL TIME SCORE

| NATURE | 1 |
| NURTURE | 1 |

NATURE V. NURTURE

So big bro and big sis can help you in your football career. Most important, however, are Mum and Dad. They influence you in two ways, whether you like it or not.

1. NATURE:

Inside every cell in our body is a catalogue of information – our genes – that determines what our body looks like, and to a certain extent how we behave. Our genes are a mixture of each of our parents' genes. This is why we quite often look like them and have the same traits. If your parents both have bright red hair, then you are quite likely to have it too. And if they are both talented at sports, then you might be too.

He was born to be a goalkeeper!

2. NURTURE:

The environment that you are born into and the way you are brought up also play a big part in who you are. If you play a lot of sport from an early age and put in hours and hours of practice, you have a better chance of making it as a professional.

So it is a combination of nature and nurture that makes us the people we are.

KEEP IT IN THE FAMILY

If one (or both) of your parents is a footballer, you will have both nature and nurture in your favour: sporty genes and a home environment where football is appreciated. Several children of professional footballers have also become professionals too. But these football families are quite rare. Of the 125 different players named in England's nine World Cup squads between 1982 and 2014, only four had dads who also played for England. That's less than 4 per cent.

PLAYER	DAD
Alex Oxlade-Chamberlain	Mark Chamberlain
Mark Hateley	Tony Hateley
Frank Lampard, Jnr	Frank Lampard, Snr
Sean Wright-Phillips	Ian Wright

Some (but not many) top players in England's Women's Super League also come from footballing families.

PLAYER	RELATION
Eniola Aluko	Sone Aluko (brother)
Natasha Dowie	Iain Dowie (uncle)
Danielle Hill	Mark Hateley (uncle)

So don't be put off your football dreams if neither your parents nor family are professional athletes. Hardly anyone else's are either.

HOW MUCH PRACTICE, MUM?

Whatever help you get from your family, continual practice is crucial to becoming an amazing footballer. The more you practise the better you will be, but how much is enough? Some people say that if you spend 10,000 hours practising anything, you will become an expert in it. That's a long time. If you spent 12 hours a day, every day, practising free kicks, you would only reach 10,000 hours after two years and three months of doing nothing else. You would have no friends and a very boring life, but you would be brilliant at free kicks.

Here are some other jobs that the 10,000-hour rule applies to:

Finally, I've reached 10,000 hours.

Ice-skater

Pianist

Master criminal

HAPPY BIRTHDAYS, UNHAPPY BIRTHDAYS

Belgian midfielder Eden Hazard had the ideal childhood for becoming a footballer. Both nature and nurture were on his side. His dad Thierry and his mum Carine were both footballers. And behind his back garden in Belgium was a field where he practised his tricks day after day. (But who knows if it was for 10,000 hours!) Hazard had one other factor that helped his aim of becoming a footballer. He was born on 7 January.

This date makes a difference because you have more chance of succeeding as a young footballer if you are born earlier in the school year and are one of the oldest in your class. In Belgium, where Hazard was born, the school year age cut-off is January 1. This means that the oldest pupils in the year are born in January and the youngest in December.

(England is a bit different – the cut-off is 1 September, so the oldest pupils are born in September, and the youngest in August.)

At school, older children are often bigger, faster and stronger than their younger classmates, since they have had a few extra months to grow. And if you are a bit bigger, faster and stronger, you are more likely to get picked for the school team, which in turn will help you improve, so you have more chances of getting picked for a football club's youth academy. This is called the **relative age effect**.

This phenomenon helps explain this curious fact: children who are born early in the school year dominate the academies of top clubs. In one season, 57 per cent of players at Premier League academies were born between September and December. Only 14 per cent were born between May and August. "Where are the May to August kids?" asked Nick Levett, the Football Association's national development manager at the time. "The simple fact is that adults have voted them out of the game because of our desire to pick bigger, stronger, faster players."

PLAYERS BORN
ON 1 JANUARY
Roberto Rivellino (Brazil)
Davor Šuker (Croatia)
Lilian Thuram (France)
Jack Wilshere (England)
Steven Davis (N. Ireland)

But it is not all good news for those who are born early in the school year. Yes, they are more likely to become a professional footballer at a young age – but they could also be more likely to get injured and end their careers earlier.

It's a bit like the fable of the hare and the tortoise. The hare sprints into an early lead, but it is the plodding tortoise that gets there in the end. Children who are born later in the school year tend to join clubs later but often have the longest careers.

ACADEMY AGES

Football clubs are only just beginning to understand how important it is to make sure that all children have a chance to make it when they are still at school age, not just the ones born early in the year. Often players who are born late in the school year slip through the net, a shame for them and their clubs.

Ajax in the Netherlands has introduced a new system to tackle this problem. Their academy doesn't split children into Under-8s, Under-9s and Under-10s. Instead it has three broader age groups: 6–11, 12–15 and 16–19. These categories mean that even those born at the beginning of the school year will sometimes be playing with older players. Each player will have a different experience: sometimes being the oldest in the age category and sometimes being the youngest. It is hoped that this will eliminate the relative age effect.

Premier League teams have also started to take note and now organize tournaments with young players picked not based on their age, but according to their physical maturity. And that's what we believe here at Football School.

Age and size should make no difference to how you do anything. If you're good, you're good!

GREVILLE AND NEVILLE

☆ STAR PUPIL

"Mamma Mia!"

☆☆☆ STAR PUPIL Stats

Siblings: 17
Age difference: 120 seconds
Freckle count (Greville): 300
Freckle count (Neville): 301
Birthplace: Mumbai, India
Support: Motherwell (Scotland)
Fave player: Ashley Young
Trick: Never forget a birthday

PHSE QUIZ

1. **France midfielder Paul Pogba's elder twin brothers, Florentin and Mathias, play for which national team?**

   a) France
   b) Guinea
   c) Ivory Coast
   d) Australia

2. **To play the game Happy Families, you need:**

   a) A special pack of cards
   b) A great-grandmother
   c) A football
   d) An open space

3. **What was unusual about the substitution of Arnor Gudjohnsen when Iceland played Estonia in 1996?**

   a) His wife was having a baby in the stands.
   b) His son Eidur replaced him.
   c) He got married on the pitch before the game.
   d) His sister was the assistant coach.

4. **What was special about Toni Vidigal, Luis Vidigal and Beto Vidigal, who played in midfield for the Portuguese side Elvas CAD in 1993?**

   a) They had the same surname but were not related.
   b) They were cousins and their uncle Victor was the coach.
   c) They were brothers.
   d) In the same season, three Vidigals also played for the local women's team, Elvenses.

5. **Alex is looking at a picture of a man and states, "Brothers and sisters have I none, but that man's father is my father's son." Who is the man in the picture?**

   a) Alex's son
   b) Alex
   c) Alex's father
   d) Ben

Football as we know it now is only about 150 years old, which for historians makes it a very recent invention. But for the thousands of years before football, people across the world played other types of ball games.

VERY RECENT.

In this lesson we are going to go back in time to look at three of these ancient sports. One is from China, one is from Japan and the other is from Central America. We'll see how all of these games contain elements of what football is today.

We're not, however, going to encourage anyone to play these sports here at Football School. The rules would require us to smear the losing team with white powder, whip them in public or chop their heads off. The classroom would get very messy!

CUJU

Where: China, Korea, Vietnam

When: From about 200 BC to AD 1400

The ball: Spherical-shaped. Originally it was stitched leather stuffed with fur or feathers, but in later years it was filled with air, a bit like balls today.

The goal: Sometimes crescent-shaped, sometimes a sheet with a hole in it suspended from two bamboo posts.

The rules: Two teams of up to sixteen players faced each other on a pitch with goals at each end. Players were not allowed to use their hands.

Kit: Long robes.

Who played: At first only soldiers in the army who spent a lot of time on horses played cuju, in order to get the blood circulating in their legs. Later the game spread to civilians and royalty; women were allowed to play. Over time, the best players were able to make a living as cuju professionals in organized leagues.

When played: At royal feasts and diplomatic events.

Winners' prize: Silver bowls or nice fabric.

Losers' prize: Their faces smeared with white powder and a public whipping.

Famous players: Emperor Wu of Han.

Spin-offs: A type of cuju with no goals, where two teams had to pass the ball to each other and were penalized for making mistakes, was also popular. Players were allowed to use any part of their body to pass the ball except their hands.

How is cuju similar to football? It was an organized game with two teams using a spherical ball, in which the aim was to score more goals than your opponent. It was very popular, with professional leagues and famous players.

What else was going on at the time? Cuju emerged at the same time that China changed from being a collection of warring states to a single empire, ruled by an emperor. In order to protect this new empire from tribes to the north, the Chinese started to build a wall that got so big and long it's now known as the Great Wall of China.

Under the rule of cuju-playing Emperor Wu of Han, who lived between 156 and 87 BC, China expanded to include parts of Korea and Vietnam.

The ancient Chinese invented many things, such as paper, steel, porcelain and gunpowder. By the time of cuju's demise, China was the most advanced civilization in the world.

KEMARI

Where: Japan
When: AD 600 to 1900
The ball: Hollow, spherical and made from deerskin.
The pitch: A square bounded by four trees, one at each corner. For this reason the game was also known as "Standing among the trees". The trees were usually a pine, a cherry, a willow and a maple.

JAPAN

TOKYO

OSAKA

Pine

Maple

Cherry

Willow

The aim: Kemari was just like playing keepy-uppy as a group. The players kicked the ball in the air as many times as they could without it touching the ground, while passing it between themselves.

The rules: Players were allowed to use their upper bodies to knock the ball down to their foot or leg. They could also bounce the ball off the trees.

Kit: Formal Japanese clothing with very large sleeves, and a rimless hat. Socks were colour-coded according to rank and skill.

Who played: Warriors and royals.

Language: When a player kicked a ball to himself, he shouted, "Ari", "Ya" or "Oh", which are the names of gods who were believed to live in the trees.

Positions: Between six and eight people played the game, standing in a circle. The best four players were each in front of one of the trees.

The game: The players walked on to the pitch in order of rank, with the highest coming on first. All players had a practice kick to get used to the ball. The game started when the player of the highest rank kicked off. The game ended when the same player kicked the ball high and caught it in his robes.

Length of a game: Usually about fifteen minutes, although an old text says that an emperor and his kemari team once kept the ball in the air for more than a 1,000 kicks.

Still around today? Yes. A few Japanese have preserved the tradition. George H. W. Bush, former president of the USA, played kemari on an official visit to Japan in 1992.

How is kemari similar to football? Kemari was a kicking game using a spherical ball that is almost identical to skill training games that footballers play today.

What else was going on at the time? From around 1100 until 1600, Japan was a country dominated by warriors called samurai. These fierce fighters had distinctive armour and were famous for their long, curved swords, their self-discipline and their code of honour. Gradually samurai principles of loyalty and duty became part of Japanese culture generally.

In the 1630s Japan's military leader banned all foreigners from entering the country and all Japanese people from leaving it. For the next 200 years Japan was almost totally disconnected from the rest of the world. During this period they kept on playing kemari. Sushi – blocks of rice with raw fish on top – was invented and activities such as puppet theatre and writing haikus also flourished around this time.

A haiku poem has three lines, with five syllables (stresses) in the first and last lines and seven in the middle line. Usually a haiku makes an observation about life or nature. Here are two we've written on our favourite subject:

Football

Everything is fun
At the Football School of joy
Then the whistle blows

No one loves football
More than Alex and Ben do
Except maybe you

PITZ

Where: Central America (the area including Mexico, Guatemala, Belize, Honduras, Nicaragua, El Salvador and Costa Rica)

When: 1500 BC to AD 1500

Who played: The Olmecs, the Maya and the Aztecs, among others.

The ball: Bouncy! The Central Americans were the first people to discover how to make rubber, which comes from latex – a milky substance found in a tree. The balls made for pitz were solid rubber and probably a bit bigger and heavier than a basketball.

CENTRaL AMERiCa
(Pre-Columbus)

TeNocHtitLaN

MaYaN CiViLiZatioN

AZteC EMPiRE

OLMEC HeaRtLaNd

The pitch: Narrower than a football pitch, and sometimes shaped like a capital I. Usually sloping stone walls were on the left and right sides of the pitch. Archaeologists, the people who study the remains of civilizations, have discovered more than 1,500. The pitch sizes vary from smaller than a tennis court to about the size of a full-length football field.

The goals: Most of the pitches didn't have goals, but towards the end of the Maya period people started to hang a stone ring high up on each of the two side walls. The idea seems to have been to get the ball through the ring, although this was probably quite difficult to do.

The rules: No one knows the rules any more, it's probable that over 3,000 years they changed a lot. The most likely theory is that two teams would face each other and bounce the ball between them using only their hips.

Kit: Pictures and sculptures from the era show that the basic kit consisted of a loincloth and a hip guard. But there were many accessories: helmets, headdresses, chest protectors, shin pads and gloves.

Dangers: The ball was very heavy and historians believe that players got bruised a lot. Some players may have died when the ball hit them in the mouth or stomach.

Purpose: The game was an important religious ritual and also sometimes used as a way of settling disputes.

Religious significance? The sacred book of the Maya is called the Popol Vuh. It had the same function as the Bible does for Christians or the Koran does for Muslims, in that it provided stories about the creation of the world.

The central story is based around a game of pitz. The two heroes are the twins Hunahpu and Xbalanque. The lords of the underworld – they're the equivalent of the devil – challenged the twins to a ball game. After many hair-raising escapades in the underworld, including the time that Hunahpu's head was chopped off by a bat and used as the ball (a turtle made him a new one), eventually Hunahpu and Xbalanque defeated the evil empire. When they re-entered the real world, the twins rose high into the sky and became the sun and the moon.

There goes Itzcali, he always loved football.

Winners' prize: Treated to a feast. **Losers' prize:** Their heads were chopped off. Some historians say that their skulls were then used as the basis of a new ball.

Still around today? Yes. The game of ulama, which is descended from pitz, is still played in a few places in Mexico.

How is pitz similar to football? Pitz was a ball game between two teams in which you were not allowed to use your hands. It was hugely popular and culturally important. Large stadiums were built to play and watch it.

What else was going on at the time? Chocolate! The cocoa bean, which is the main ingredient in chocolate, is native to the Americas and was made into a drink enjoyed all over Central America. It tasted very different from the chocolate we eat now because the Maya and the Aztecs didn't have sugar. Instead, they mixed ground cocoa beans with water, chilli peppers and cornmeal. Yuk!

MAYA GOLDBERG

☆ STAR PUPIL

66 Watch your head! 99

☆☆☆ STAR PUPIL | Stats

Age: 2,578 years
Number of rubber trees in garden: 1
Collection of headdresses: 14
Goals scored through the ring: 1
Birthplace: Oldham, England
Supports: Newell's Old Boys (Argentina)
Fave Stadium: Estadio Azteca
Trick: Shoots from the hip
☆

HISTORY QUIZ

1. **What did the ancient Chinese build along their northern border that is thousands of miles long?**

   a) A running track
   b) A wall
   c) A zip wire
   d) A football pitch

2. **Which of these countries is situated where the Maya used to live?**

   a) Greenland
   b) Great Britain
   c) Guatemala
   d) Japan

3. **The samurai sword was special in what way?**

   a) It was straight.
   b) It had two blades.
   c) It had a long grip for both hands.
   d) It was made of gold.

4. **Which of the following did the Chinese NOT invent?**

   a) Toothpaste
   b) Printing
   c) Silk
   d) The compass

5. **The Olmecs were the first major civilization in Central America. What does their name mean?**

   a) Rubber people
   b) Fierce people
   c) Ball people
   d) Chosen people

BALL person →

PSYCHOLOGY

Scoring a penalty should be easy. You place the ball on the white spot a few metres in front of the goal and then kick it, with only the goalkeeper standing in your way.

But penalties are not that easy.

Some of the best players in the world, including Alex's friend Pelé, have missed important penalties. Argentinian midfielder Diego Maradona, one of football's best ever players, once missed five penalties in a row!

Luckily we have a world expert on penalties here at Football School. Ben spent two years studying everything there is to know about penalties, and even wrote a brilliant book on them. In this lesson he will reveal his five top tips to score the perfect penalty.

It's good that we're in the classroom and not out on the pitch, because the overwhelming message is that when it comes to penalty kicks, the most important part of your body is not your foot, but your brain.

ON THE SPOT
Penalties happen when:
1. The referee believes a foul or a handball has taken place in the penalty area.
2. A knockout game ends with the score level after extra time. Then there is a penalty shoot-out – each team takes five penalties and whoever scores the most wins.

BEN'S TIPS FOR
THE PERFECT PENALTY

Imagine you are about to take a penalty in front of a stadium packed full of fans. Follow these top tips from Ben and learn how to be at the top of your mental game.

BEN'S TIP No. 1
BE POSITIVE

Read this carefully: I want you to clear your mind from thinking about elephants.

Absolutely do NOT think about elephants.

Especially a pink elephant in a tutu.

Are we ready? I bet you are thinking about a pink elephant in a tutu.

You are having these thoughts because it is impossible for humans to *not* think about something that has been suggested to them. We can't do it!

In the same way, if you are about to take a penalty you should not say to yourself, "I must not miss, I must not miss." Because thinking about NOT missing is the same as thinking about missing.

And you don't want to be thinking about missing, because then you will be more likely to miss. When you take a penalty you want to be thinking about scoring.

In order not to fill your mind with thoughts about missing, **focus** hard on what you are doing – for example, counting the steps in your run-up. And think, "I will score."

MY ALL-TIME TOP FIVE PENALTY TAKERS

1. Matt Le Tissier (England)
Scored 47 out of 48 penalties in his career

2. Gaizka Mendieta (Spain)
Always waited for the keeper to move — then went the other way

3. Antonín Panenka (Czech Republic)
Invented a slow lobbed penalty down the middle of the goal — now called the "Panenka" in his honour

4. Brandi Chastain (USA)
Took a penalty to win the 1999 Women's World Cup final

5. Zinedine Zidane (France)
Usually kicked to his right side — but hit it so accurately it was virtually unstoppable

BEN'S TIP No. 2
TAKE YOUR TIME

England have two world records when it comes to penalties:

1. England miss more penalties in shoot-outs than any other national team.
2. Once the ref blows their whistle, England players take their penalties quicker on average than any other country.

Do you think these two records are related? Of course they are! Rushing can lead to mistakes, in life and in football.

So my advice is this: once the ref blows their whistle, be calm. **Don't rush. Take an extra breath. Compose yourself.** Make sure you are ready. And then take the penalty.

Team spirit is really important for staying positive. You need to feel it in the good times and the bad. In fact, you need it more when things get bad.

So if a player misses a penalty, don't get angry with them. Walk up to them, **give them a hug** and say nice things to them.

Trust me: teams that celebrate goals and hug players who miss in a penalty shoot-out are more likely to win the penalty shoot-out.

If players know that they will still be loved by their team even if they miss, they become less scared of missing and therefore more likely to score.

BEN'S TIP No. 4
KEEP EYE CONTACT WITH THE KEEPER

Once the ball is on the penalty spot, you need to mark out your run-up. You have two choices. Either you can walk backwards, while always keeping an eye on the goal and the goalkeeper, or you can walk with your back to the keeper before turning around to face the ball.

Most England players walk with their back to the keeper, thus avoiding eye contact with him. And we know that lots of England players miss!

Some psychologists think that avoiding eye contact shows fear and gives the goalkeeper an advantage. Instead, it's better to face the challenge head-on. **Keep eye contact**. Let your opponent think you are confident. That will make *them* start worrying!

BEN'S TIP No. 5
PRACTISE WITH PURPOSE

When England lost a penalty shoot-out to Italy in Euro 2012, England coach Roy Hodgson said that practising penalties before the game had been no help: "You can't reproduce the pressure. You can't reproduce the nervous tension." Previous England coaches have said something very similar.

They are right. You can't.

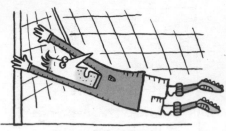

But the same is true of most sports: you can never copy the exact conditions for a tennis player serving to win Wimbledon, or a golfer putting to win the Ryder Cup, or a cyclist scaling a hill climb at the Tour de France. But those athletes still practise, don't they?

In fact, a tennis player, a golfer and a cyclist all told me the same thing: they practise with purpose. That means they pretend the situation is exactly the same, even if it isn't. They try to copy the conditions as much as possible. A cyclist won't practise a hill climb on a flat road, will they? They'll find a hill and climb it! And they'll make it competitive, with prizes for winning and forfeits for losing.

That's how players can practise for penalties – with purpose. So that means taking penalties at the end of a game when you're tired. It means practising the long walk from the centre circle to the penalty spot in a shoot-out. It means waiting for the referee to blow the whistle and imagining the world is watching. **Preparation for anything will increase your chances of success**. Penalties are no different!

In fact, we think you can handle tricky situations in life in the same way you handle penalties.

Anytime you face a tough challenge, use this handy summary of Ben's five tips to help you.

They work from the penalty spot on the pitch, so why not off the pitch too?

1. Focus
2. Don't rush
3. Be supportive
4. Look the challenge in the eye
5. Be prepared

BEN'S Referee's Little Black Book

MY ALL-TIME TOP FIVE PENALTY SHOOT-OUTS

West Germany 5 France 4 (1982 World Cup semi-final)
The first World Cup shoot-out, and the first on live TV.

Brazil 3 Italy 2 (1994 World Cup final)
The world's best player at the time, Robert Baggio, missed the final penalty and Italy lost.

KK Palace 17 Civics 16 (2005 Namibian Cup Final)
It took a world-record 48 kicks for this shoot-out to end.

Liverpool 3 AC Milan 2 (2005 Champions League final)
The Reds' keeper Jerzy Dudek waved his arms to put off kickers.

Netherlands U21 13 England U21 12
(2007 European Under-21 Championship semi-final)
Netherlands' body language expert told players to give positive signals.

TWELVE YARDS

Often commentators will talk about the penalty spot being twelve yards from the goal. The yard is an old-fashioned unit of measurement that seems only to be used when talking about distances in sport.

Twelve inches make a foot, and three feet make a yard. So the penalty spot is 36 feet from the goal, or 432 inches.

Nowadays we tend to use the metric system of measurement for distances. Twelve yards is equal to 10.97 metres, which is almost eleven metres.

In German the word for penalty is "elfmeter", which translates as "eleven metres", since "elf" is the German word for eleven. So "elfmeter" has nothing to do with measuring Santa's little helpers!

BRIAN POWER

☆ STAR PUPIL

" Heads up! "

STAR PUPIL stats

Positive thoughts per game: 86
Steps in run-up: 11
Length of wait before taking penalty: 5.6 seconds
Average penalty speed: 58 mph
Birthplace: Braintree, England
Supports: Penafiel (Portugal)
Fave player: Tom Cleverley
Trick: Impossible to tell which way he will shoot

PSYCHOLOGY QUIZ

1. **What is a penalty that is slowly chipped down the middle of the goal called?**

a) Zidane
b) Panenka
c) Unlucky
d) Le Tissier

2. **What happens if the scores are level in a penalty shoot-out after both teams have taken five penalties?**

a) The coaches take penalties.
b) They keep going until one team misses and the other scores.
c) The captains play scissors-paper-stone.
d) They toss a coin.

3. **What was special about Martin Palermo's performance for Argentina in a 1999 Copa América game against Colombia?**

a) He scored three penalties.
b) He missed three penalties.
c) He scored a penalty and saved a penalty.

d) He broke the crossbar with a penalty.

4. **What did French midfielder Zinedine Zidane do before scoring a penalty against England at Euro 2004?**

a) Kissed the referee
b) Sang the French national anthem, "La Marseillaise"
c) Vomited on the edge of the penalty area
d) Shook the hands of all his teammates for luck

5. **Why is Alex Molodetsky famous in the world of penalties?**

a) He trained elephants to score penalties.
b) He once scored a penalty with his head.
c) He could save penalties blindfolded.
d) He invented a ball that veers into the goal even if it's aimed off target.

DESIGN TECHNOLOGY

Wednesday
Lesson 1+2

In the last lesson we forgot to mention another essential element in penalty-taking. Indeed this element is essential for all parts of the game. If you want to play well, you need a good pair of boots.

Imagine playing in boots that went over your ankles. They would be heavier than the boots you play in today. You would run more slowly and use up more energy. Not great!

Yet that is what football boots were like up until the 1950s.

Shoemakers today put a lot of thought into the design of football boots and the materials they use to make them. In this lesson we are going to see how the design of boots has changed over time. But first, let's see just what a difference the right boots can make to a game.

STUDS-U-LIKE

Hungary were big favourites to win the 1954 World Cup final against West Germany in Bern, Switzerland. But the Mighty Magyars lost 3–2, handing the Germans their first World Cup trophy. Many commentators said the Germans' victory was down to their football boots, which had screw-in studs. It rained heavily and the pitch was muddy: the Germans were able to screw in larger studs to their regular boots, giving them an advantage on the slippy turf. After that game everyone in football realized just how important it is to have the right boots.

A HIS-TOE-RY OF FOOTIE FOOTWEAR

1500s:

King Henry VIII owned one of the earliest pairs of boots specifically made for playing football. We know he had a pair because they were listed in a palace document as having been made by his personal shoemaker, Cornelius Johnson, in 1526. Historians think the

boots were ankle-high, made from strong leather and heavier than normal boots. In the Tudor period football wasn't the game we play today, but a kind of organized brawl that often led to riots. Off the pitch, Henry VIII could be ruthless: he had six wives and chopped the heads off two of them. So pity anyone who got in his way during a game.

1850-1900:

The first boots designed solely for modern football were made from thick leather and had leather studs to grip the turf. They were heavy and doubled in weight when wet.

1900-50:

Famous boot producers, such as Gola in the UK and hummel in Germany, opened for business. One big German company, the Dassler Brothers Shoe Factory, introduced replaceable studs that could be changed depending on the weather. Later the company split into two.

1950s:

Brazilian designers removed the ankle part of the football boot. English forward Stanley Matthews saw Brazil play in the 1950 World Cup and bought a pair of their boots. He returned home and asked the Heckmondwike Boot and Shoe Works to copy them. The lower-cut design was lighter, allowing players to run faster.

1960-70:

Leather was replaced by lighter materials such as rubber. In 1970 English midfielder Alan Ball became the first player to wear white boots.  He was paid £2,000 by hummel to do so. But hummel didn't have a pair that fit, so the marketing director painted Ball's adidas boots white and then added chevrons to make them look like a hummel boot.

1980s:

Liverpool ex-midfielder Craig Johnston wanted to help kids he was coaching control the ball better. He designed a new boot, the Adidas Predator, which had rubber fins to help that. The Predator is still worn today. Other boot designers followed his lead.

2000-PRESENT:

In recent years new technology has inspired lots of weird and wacky boots. These include boots without laces and boots made using sharkskin leather, with holes in the soles like gills.

I love my shark-skin boots!

MATERIAL WORLD

Football boots need to be many things. They need to be comfy, so players enjoy wearing them. They need to be tough, so the feet are protected. They need to be hard-wearing, so they don't fall apart in the middle of a game, and they need to be light, so they don't weigh players down. These factors decide the many different materials that go into the modern boot.

That is boot-i-ful.

The studs are the hardest part of a boot. The stud's job is to penetrate the ground so that you can grip instead of slipping. The material must be unbendable, unbreakable and tough. Studs are usually made from a light metal such as **aluminium**, or a hard **plastic**, or a mixture of both.

The sole of a boot has to be stiff enough to keep the studs in place, flexible enough so that it doesn't shatter when you run and hard enough to protect the foot. The most suitable material is a light plastic, but one that is more flexible than the hard plastic used for studs. Some boots use a plastic that only bends in one direction, since the extra stiffness that you get from it not bending in the other direction can increase the power of a kick.

The upper of the boot covers the sides and top of your foot. It needs to be flexible so you can control the ball and so it's comfy when you run. The material also has to be

tough so you are
protected if you
are trodden on,
and so it doesn't
get damaged when
you kick the ball. **Leather** is
best for this job, as it is very

hard-wearing and performs well in all temperatures
and weather conditions. Scientists have invented many
amazing materials, but when it comes to boots nothing is as
versatile as the skin of a cow.

Modern boots also have plastic ridges and skins on the
upper that create texture to help you control the ball.

HAPPY FEET

The best players in the world don't have to go shopping for football boots: bootmakers give them pairs for free.

When you play football every day, your feet develop extra muscle in the toes. In order to protect this muscle and not be too tight, professional footballers' boots sometimes have more padding around the toes. And what's more, the bootmakers take a mould of each player's feet and use them to make boots that will fit perfectly, like a second skin. Argentinian forward Lionel Messi says he likes his boots to "feel more like slippers than shoes". Maybe he should wear a dressing-gown too!

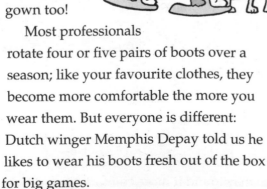

Most professionals rotate four or five pairs of boots over a season; like your favourite clothes, they become more comfortable the more you wear them. But everyone is different: Dutch winger Memphis Depay told us he likes to wear his boots fresh out of the box for big games.

PIMP MY BOOT

Often players like to personalise the design of their boots with words or images:

PLAYER	BOOTMAKER	PERSONALISATION
Pierre-Emerick Aubameyang	Nike	Encrusted with 4,000 Swarovski crystals and his initials, PEA
Lionel Messi	adidas	Sons' names and Argentina flag
Mario Balotelli	Puma	Fake mohawk hairstyle on the heel
Neymar	Nike	"Courage" and "joy" on side, NJR11 on the heel
Memphis Depay	Under Armour	"Memphis" signature on the heel

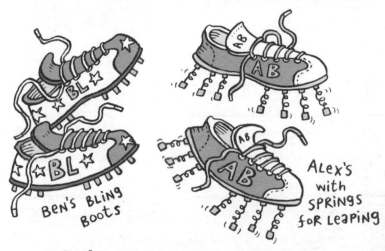

Ben's Bling Boots

Alex's with springs for leaping

DON'T TREAD ON MY TOES

Not all players like to wear boots. India were invited to play in the 1950 World Cup but did not turn up after the organizers, FIFA, said that all players had to wear football boots. India's team had played in the 1948 Olympics with some of their players wearing only bandages on their feet, as they found it more comfortable (and lighter) that way.

FAMILY FEUD

Adidas and Puma are two of the biggest sports brands, but did you know they were founded by two brothers who hated each other? Adi and Rudolf Dassler started the Dassler Brothers Shoe Factory in the 1920s. But the brothers fell out and in 1948 Adi established adidas and Rudolf set up a company that became Puma. The two factories were in the same town in Germany, on opposite sides of the river. The brothers never became friends again.

"SPEEDY" STEVIE FINS

★ STaR PUPIL

66 Eat my boots! 99

☆
☆☆ STaR PUPIL | StatS

Swerve factor: 180 degrees
Top speed: 100 mph
Boots: 100 pairs
Smart shoes: 1 pair
Birthplace: Bootle, England
Supports: Boston Red Sox (American baseball)
Fave player: Wilfried Bony
Trick: Ball sticks to his shoes

DESIGN TECHNOLOGY QUIZ

1. What is the name of the top part of a boot?

a) The downer
b) The middler
c) The upper
d) The topper

2. Which of these is a desirable property of the sole of a football boot?

a) Elastic
b) Porous
c) Aromatic
d) Rigid

3. Why do referees check players' studs before they come on the pitch?

a) To make sure they don't have chewing gum on their soles
b) To ensure the studs are not sharp or dangerous to opponents

c) To check that both shoes have the same number studs
d) It's a tradition dating back to horse-drawn carts, when drivers used to check horses' hooves.

4. What would be the most sensible material for boot laces from the ones below?

a) Cotton
b) Rubber
c) Spaghetti
d) Straw

5. Which of these football boots does NOT exist?

a) Hypervenom
b) Mercurial Vapor
c) Evo Goal 90
d) Purple Power Cat

GEOGRAPHY

For this lesson we're going to fly down to Brazil, the most successful country in international football. Brazil has won the World Cup more times than anyone else: in 1958, 1962, 1970, 1994 and 2002.

Brazil has also produced more top footballers than any other nation, and they continue to sell more professional players around the world than anyone else.

So how come the Brazilians are so good? What have they got that no one else has? Alex used to live in Rio de Janeiro, and this is what he found out.

BIG IS BEAUTIFUL

Brazil is the largest country in South America. It's massive – you could fit the UK into it about 33 times.

It is also full of people – there are almost as many Brazilians as there are people in the UK, France and Germany put together. So that's one reason there are lots of Brazilian footballers: there are lots of Brazilians.

BRaZiL is Huge!

AMaZoN RIVER

AMaZoN RaiN foRest

BRaSiLia

RIO

São PauLo

south AMERica

If you look at how many people live in each country in the world, you can see that Brazil is in the top five:

COUNTRY	POPULATION	% OF WORLD POPULATION
China	1.4 billion	20%
India	1.3 billion	19%
USA	324 million	5%
Indonesia	258 million	4%
Brazil	206 million	3%

TROPICAL TURF TROUBLES

Brazil also has lots of animals. In fact, it has more species of animal than anywhere else in the world, including armadillos, monkeys, sloths and vampire bats. This variety is called **biodiversity** and is due to Brazil being a tropical country with many different habitats, such as the Amazon rainforest, desert, savannah and swamps. The climate is nearly always hot, and the weather alternates between blistering sun and torrential rain storms.

When it comes to football, Brazilians tend to be very skilful players. They are known for their ball control and their repertoire of tricks. Believe it or not, the extreme weather plays an important part in this.

Thunderous downpours and scorching heat are brilliant for the plants that live in the rainforest – but terrible for grass.

In Brazil it is almost impossible to maintain a grass lawn … or a football pitch. In fact, the country has almost NO grass football pitches. Schools don't have grass fields for children to practise on and there are very few parks. The very few grass pitches that there are in Brazil are mostly in stadiums, where gardeners have to tend them every day.

You might think that because almost no young Brazilians learn to play on grass they would be WORSE, not better footballers, but, as we will see, the opposite is the case.

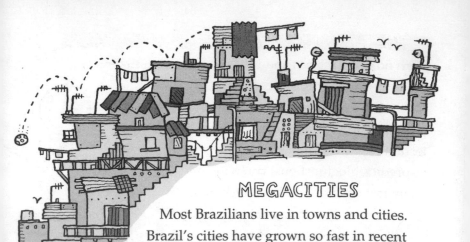

MEGACITIES

Most Brazilians live in towns and cities. Brazil's cities have grown so fast in recent decades that many of them have several million people in them. The biggest city, São Paulo, has almost as many people living in it as the whole of Australia does.

These megacities are crammed full of people, with few large open spaces for people to run around on (apart from the beach, if the city has one). In the poorest parts of these cities there are almost no roads: simple brick homes are built on top of each other with only tiny pathways between them. There is hardly any space to swing a cat, let alone kick a ball. But the Brazilians use this to their advantage too.

POPULATION OF BIGGEST CITIES

Brasília (the capital) 4 million	Porto Alegre 4 million	Belo Horizonte 5 million	Rio de Janeiro 12 million	São Paulo 20 million

THE ADVANTAGES OF DISADVANTAGES

With no grass pitches and little space in cities to play football, instead people learn the game on patches of dirt and on the street.

If you are playing on gnarled, knobbly terrain where the ball will bounce in unpredictable directions, you will develop really fast reactions and good technique.

If you are playing on concrete where you can't fall without hurting yourself, you will develop amazing control and balance. If you are playing football in tiny spaces, you will develop brilliant ball skills.

Rough terrain

CoNCRete

TiNY Space

In other words, one of the reasons why Brazil's footballers are so good is because the geography – that's the climate and the cities – provides so many obstacles to playing.

A PITCH WITH A DIFFERENCE

There are two other places where the Brazilians find space to play football, and they are also important:

1. INDOORS

Because of the lack of outdoor pitches, many young Brazilians learn to play football indoors on a hard court floor. The indoor game is called futsal. It is five-a-side football played on a pitch roughly the size of a basketball court and using a smaller, heavier ball.

Because the futsal ball does not bounce very well, it requires much more technique to master. Futsal players have less space to move around in than footballers on a full-sized pitch, which means that futsal players have to be very quick, with better close ball control and no fear of dribbling. The result is that if you play futsal, you become a fast and fearless player.

Futsal was invented in Uruguay, Brazil's neighbour, but the game became more popular in Brazil than anywhere else. In fact, more Brazilians play futsal than play football.

Brazil even has a professional futsal league. Many of the country's best players started out playing futsal. Now we know why they are so good!

StaR fuTsaLLeRs

Marta
Neymar
Pelé
Ronaldinho
Zico

2. THE BEACH

Brazil has about 5,000 miles of coastline and beaches cover much of it. There are beaches in many of Brazil's major cities – such as Rio de Janeiro, Santos, Salvador and Recife – and football gets played on them.

Beach football is much harder to play than normal football because you need more energy to run on sand. Since the ball hardly bounces you have to be much more accurate with passes, and also use lots of different parts of your body to control the ball. So if you play beach football, you will be very fit and have great technique.

DANCING OFF THE PITCH

As well as the sun, the rain, the cities, the indoor courts and the beaches, Brazilians have another big advantage when it comes to football – they love to dance. Brazil's national musical style is called samba. Samba is very fast, uplifting and rhythmical, and is usually played on percussion instruments such as small drums, shakers and the tambourine. Samba also has its own special style of dancing, in which you tap your feet and wiggle your hips a lot. Children growing up in Brazil learn how to samba, so they learn to move their feet and shake their hips much better than children in other countries. Wiggling your hips is very useful in football also – for wiggling past defenders and twisting your body to strike the ball.

WHO NEEDS A BALL ANYWAY?

Brazil has many families who are too poor to buy a football for their children to play with. Lots of people told Alex that it's common for children from these families to learn to play football using coconuts, oranges and even eggs.

If you learn to play football with a coconut you are going to get sore feet. If you learn with an orange you are going to get sticky feet.

And if you learn with an egg, someone is going to get splatted!

But there are advantages to using such unconventional (and tasty) objects as footballs. It is much more difficult to play football with fruit than it is with a nice pumped-up ball, so children who learn with unusual objects are going to develop better ball skills. Imagine trying to do keepy-uppies with an egg! (We do not suggest you do this at home.) You will need to have an almost insane level of control to kick and catch the egg without it breaking.

So when we look at Brazil, we can see that for aspiring footballers, adversity breeds creativity. This means that the greater a challenge is, the more resourceful you need to be to overcome it. Young Brazilians are faced with many challenges when it comes to playing football, and as a result they develop amazing, world-beating skills.

In 1953 Brazil launched a competition to design the national team's strip. The winning entry of a yellow jersey with green collar and cuffs — which is still worn today — was sent in by a teenager who had never designed a football strip before!

SMITHZINHO

☆ STAR PUPIL

"God is Brazilian!"

☆☆☆ STAR PUPIL | STATS

Daily intake of coconuts: 5
Keepy-uppy record: 7,563
Number of "o"s in goooooooooooal: 10
Biodiversity of garden: 17 species of monkey, 250 species of cockroach and 1 sloth
Birthplace: Copacabana
Team: Anyone but Argentina
Fave player: Rio Ferdinand
☆ Trick: Can dance around players

GEOGRAPHY QUIZ

1. What is the capital of Brazil?

a) Belo Horizonte
b) Brasília
c) Rio de Janeiro
d) São Paulo

2. The biggest club in São Paulo, Brazil's largest city, is named after which British team?

a) Corinthians
b) Wanderers
c) The Spartans
d) Rangers

3. What is the name of the razor-toothed Amazon fish that likes to eat raw flesh and is strong enough to bite your finger off?

a) Anaconda
b) Caiman

c) South American Finger-Muncher
d) Piranha

4. What is the full name of FIFA Player of the Century Pelé?

a) Ronaldo de Assis Moreira
b) Mário Jorge Lobo Zagallo
c) Edson Arantes do Nascimento
d) Diego Armando Maradona Franco

5. Brazil's flag is a blue circle inside a gold rhombus on a green background. But what is in the blue circle?

a) 1 military cross
b) 5 footballs
c) 8 scorpions
d) 27 white stars

DRAMA

In some ways footballers are like famous actors. People pay to see them perform live. You can watch them on prime-time telly. They feature in adverts and in celebrity magazines. And, on the pitch, they also do a lot of acting.

In this lesson we are going to look at the different ways footballers act. There's both good and bad acting. Everyone loves the player or team who celebrates their goal with a jubilant piece of theatre. On the other hand, fans and commentators criticize players who scream in pretend agony when they are not really hurt.

We'll see how football often involves acting without words and how, sometimes, the game is as dramatic as the plays of ancient Greece – although you don't need to wear a toga to enjoy this lesson.

THE GOAL CELEBRATION OSCAR

First, let's look at some of the best celebrations in football. To do this, we have to go all the way to Iceland and a small team called Stjarnan. Thanks to some inspirational acting, for a brief moment this team was among the most famous in the world.

At the time the team were playing in Iceland's first division. The players were friends as well as teammates, since they had all grown up in a small town called Garðabær and had played together for over a dozen years. In Iceland they were already famous for their funny goal celebrations – but then one elaborate performance caught the whole world's imagination.

In a game against rivals Fylkir, striker Halldor Orri Bjornsson scored a match-winning penalty in the last minute. He ran to the edge of the area. He stretched out one arm as though he was casting out a fishing-rod. His teammate, Johann Laxdal, fell onto his side about six metres away. As Bjornsson pretended to reel him in with his other hand, Laxdal flopped towards him bouncing on his shoulder and hip like a fish out of water. Laxdal was apparently chosen for the role because in Icelandic, "laxdal" means "valley of the salmon".

There was more to come. Once Laxdal had flopped at the goalscorer's feet, four more teammates lifted him up and held him on his side, as though showing off their catch for a photo.  Another teammate, Baldvin Sturluson, got down on one knee and pretended to take a photo of the "salmon". The celebration was inevitably named "The Salmon". A video of it went viral and was watched by millions around the world, showing football and drama make for a great match.

Planning sequences of movement in this way is known as **choreography**. Stjarnan continued to celebrate their goals with choreographed theatrical flourishes. Here are some of their highlights. Action!

STJARNAN CELEBRATIONS

1. The Toilet – One player goes down on all fours, with two others behind him (they are the seat and flusher). The scorer sits on the back of the crouching player, pretends to read a newspaper, then stands up and pulls the hand of the flusher.

STJARNAN Toilet Celeb-Ration

2. The Bicycle – Two players kneel on the ground with one lying in between them. The back player puts his hands on the front player's shoulders. The scorer jumps on the back player's shoulders and pedals, using the player on the floor.

3. The Diver – One player kneels on the ground and the goalscorer dives off his back into an imaginary swimming pool and swims.

4. The Ballroom Dancers – The goalscorer grabs his nearest teammate and dances a waltz with him. Six other teammates pair up and do the same dance.

5. The Bobsled – Four players push an imaginary bar in the same direction, then sit in a line with legs outstretched. They lean left and then right as though in a bobsled.

STJARNAN

ACTIONS SPEAK LOUDER THAN WORDS

There are other effective ways of acting on a pitch. When we watch football on TV or even in a stadium, we can't hear what the players are saying. But we know what they are thinking, because their bodies give it away. This is called **body language**. It's a way of communicating without words and is an important tool of an actor's trade.

The defender who puts the palms of his hands together and waves them in the direction of the referee? He wants justice. The striker who storms over and puts his nose right next to his opponent's nose? He is angry.

Sometimes our bodies respond in a natural way: we smile when we are happy, we grimace or cry out when we are hurt. But in a competitive environment like a football match, some players exaggerate their reactions to events. They are doing just what clowns in the circus do: overemphasizing their facial expressions and body gestures in order to communicate wordlessly. This is a type of acting called **mime**. Players use the techniques of mime so the other players, the referee and the fans can understand their feelings on the pitch without them having to speak.

Here are some acting expressions that all footballers know (and also know how to exaggerate them for maximum effect):

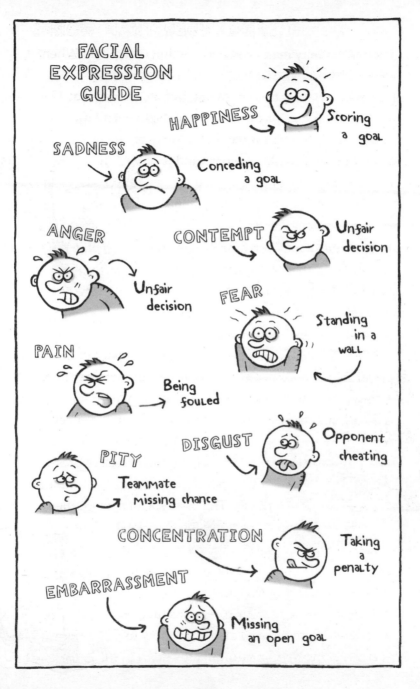

CROWD CHORUS

Footballers may behave like actors, but watching a football match is different from watching a play or a film. When you are in the theatre, cinema or just watching TV at home, usually you want silence so you can hear what is going on.

Football is the opposite. You want to be noisy, because it means you are part of the action. If you're watching a game at a stadium and singing loudly enough, the players can hear you, which can inspire them to play well and distract their opponents.

Sometimes fans boo a player if they used to play for their team in the past, or if they foul someone, or if they just have had a bad haircut. These noises from the crowd – cheers for the heroes, boos for the villains – are a way of commenting on the main characters in the action.

This used to happen in the very first plays, that were performed in ancient Greece nearly 3,000 years ago. During a play, a group of actors called the **chorus** would stand near the stage and provide a commentary on the action. They might sing a song to describe what a character is thinking, or move the plot along by adding information. So think about it the next time you go to a match: your words can also become the story. That makes you an important part of the game.

Who are ya?

DIVING COMPETITION

But perhaps the most common form of acting during a football game is when a player pretends they have been fouled to try to gain an advantage, either by winning a free kick or a penalty, or getting their opponent sent off.

This tactic is called diving. A player falls to the ground and writhes in agony. Their teammates protest that the victim was pushed or kicked. Once the referee has made a decision, the player stands up, not looking so injured after all.

A survey of the first 32 games played at the 2014 World Cup revealed that of the 302 players who collapsed on the pitch during the tournament, only nine were injured. That's about 3%. Most players were fibbing when they fell.

Many players claim they never dive, but chances are they have. Former England striker Michael Owen admitted that it's a bit of a grey area. "I don't think that in my career I ever actually dived," he said in an interview. "I certainly went down on occasions. Two of the biggest were against Argentina at World Cups, in 1998 and 2002. I went to ground in situations where it would have been just about possible for me to stay on my feet."

Referees can punish dives with a yellow card. The official term for the offence is "simulation". Writer Dave Eggers said that diving is "essentially a combination of acting, lying, begging and cheating, and these four behaviours make for an unappealing mix." At Football School, we don't like it either.

Target

THREE FAMOUS FOOTBALL FAKES

1. Roberto Rojas (Brazil v. Chile, 1989)

The Chilean goalkeeper was banned for life after pretending that he had been injured by a firecracker that had been thrown onto the pitch. He dived into the smoke of the firecracker and emerged bleeding, but it turned out that he had cut himself using a razor blade in his gloves.

2. Rivaldo (Brazil v. Turkey, 2002)

Turkish defender Hakan Ünsal kicked the ball at Rivaldo's leg and the Brazilian midfielder fell down clutching his face. Ünsal was sent off but Rivaldo was later fined.

3. Arjen Robben (Netherlands v. Mexico, 2014)

The Dutch winger apologized after trying to win a penalty by diving in the first half of a tense World Cup tie.

HOLLY WOOD

STAR PUPIL

"Break a leg!"

STAR PUPIL STATS

Most rolls to win a foul: 14
Different goal celebrations: 43
Bookings for play-acting: 9
Most kit changes in a game: 17
Birthplace: Fakenham, England
Supports: West Ham (UK)
Fave player: Craig Shakespeare
Trick: Inspiring team-talks

DRAMA QUIZ

1. Which of these celebrations did Stjarnan players once attempt after scoring a goal?

a) The Bicycle
b) The Volcano
c) The Cha-Cha-Cha
d) The Moonwalk

2. Closing your fist and keeping one thumb up is the symbol for what in most countries?

a) That's great
b) The number one
c) Do you have any nail scissors?
d) Look, my thumb cannot bend

3. What do actors traditionally say to each other before going on-stage?

a) "Sorry for farting!"
b) "Break a leg!"
c) "Don't forget your lines!"
d) "I love you darling!"

4. A bad actor, or one who over-acts, can be called a:

a) Bacon
b) Pig
c) Ham
d) Sausage

5. Which masks did Gabonese forward Pierre-Emerick Aubameyang and his teammate Marco Reus wear to celebrate the striker's goal for Borussia Dortmund against rivals Schalke?

a) Batman and Robin
b) Tom and Jerry
c) Spiderman and Superman
d) Mickey and Minnie Mouse

PHILOSOPHY

Philosophers are thinkers who ask deep questions about the meaning of life. Like René Descartes, who in 1637 said, "Cogito, ergo sum," which is Latin for, "I think, therefore I am."

cogito, ergo sum.

That's why the Football School motto is Kickito, Ergo Sum, which is made-up Latin for, "I kick, therefore I am."

Football School

Kickito Ergo Sum

A set of rules that guide you is called a philosophy, and you don't need to speak Latin or have been dead for centuries to have one. Ben's philosophy for life is: be yourself; love your family; tell jokes; eat pizza; take penalties. Alex's is: have fun; be a good friend; go cycling; do your times tables; pick your nose.

Footballers can also have philosophies for how they play. For example a philosophy could be: always attack; keep the ball on the ground; never dive.

4x6 = 24
5x6 = 30
6x6 = 36...

And coaches will have sets of rules for how they approach training and tactics. In this lesson, we will tell the story of the coach Rinus Michels, whose philosophy revolutionized football. We'll see how the vision he had half a century ago still impacts the game today.

A COACH IS BORN

Marinus "Rinus" Michels was born in Amsterdam, in the Netherlands, in 1928. He dreamt of becoming a footballer,

RiNUS MicheLS

and for his ninth birthday his dad gave him his first pair of football boots and the white-and-red kit of Ajax, who at that time were a semi-professional side.

Michels' dream came true when he was eighteen and he started playing for Ajax as a centre-forward. In his debut match in 1946 he scored five times. He was regarded as a real team player, as he worked hard and always put his team first. Although he was thought to be a little clumsy with the ball at his feet, he always kept moving and was brilliant at heading. In the 269 goals he played for Ajax, he scored 121 goals. He also played five games for the Netherlands, before he retired with an injured back, aged 30.

With his playing career over, Michels became a gymnastics teacher at a school for deaf children. Accounts say Michels was a very strict teacher. During these years he developed strategies for how to get the best out of people. Then Michels had a brainwave: why not combine his teaching skills and love of football by becoming a football coach? So in January 1965, when he learned that Ajax wanted a new coach, he applied for the job and got it.

teaching
skiLLS

football
coach

Love of
football

When he took over as coach, Ajax were struggling in the league. But in their first game with Michels in charge they won 9–3. The club not only avoided relegation, but the next year went on to win the Dutch Championship, and the one the year after that, and the one after that. Three in a row! In 1971, Ajax won the European Cup (the competition now called the Champions League) for the best team in Europe. No club has ever come from such a low point – either before then or since – to win this famous trophy.

THE GENERAL'S PHILOSOPHY

So how did Michels do it? He had a new approach to football and a new philosophy for the game. First, he was tough on his team and strict about discipline. His players nicknamed him "The General" because he set up four training sessions every day to get his team as fit as possible.

Most clubs would have one or two sessions per day, not four. Michels also introduced new tactics borrowed from other countries. He made his defenders attack, like they did in Brazil, and he encouraged his players to rotate positions, like they did in Hungary. So if a midfielder moved to the wing, the winger would replace him in midfield. This versatile new way of playing became known as "total football". These changes had amazing results.

Total football

A THINKING MAN'S TROPHIES

After his success at Ajax, Michels went to coach Barcelona in Spain, where he continued to use his innovative training methods and tactics. Under his guidance, Barcelona won the Spanish league for the first time in fourteen years.

He was then made coach of the Dutch national side. At that time, the Netherlands (often called Holland) had a mediocre team. When Michels was younger he had played for his country, but they never won, once even losing 6–1 to Sweden. But as a coach he turned them into one of the best teams in the world. They narrowly lost the 1974 World Cup final to West Germany. Later, he led his country to the only football trophy the Netherlands have ever won: the 1988 European Championship. What an incredible achievement! In 1999 Michels was named FIFA Coach of the Century.

Michels' winning formula

Top fitness and
    discipline
        +
Attacking defenders = WINNERS
        +
Rotating positions

LASTING LEGACY

Rinus Michels is important in the history
of football not only because he won lots of
trophies, but also because he left a legacy.

A legacy is something handed down through
the generations, like the vase your mum is always
telling you not to touch, or a picture of your grandparents
when they were children.

It doesn't have to be an object: it can be your auntie's
bad breath or, in this case, a way of doing things.

Michels' legacy is his philosophy of "total
football", in which a team always has
defenders who attack and players
who can swap positions. Let's take a
look at how the way Barcelona play
today is a consequence of Michels'
work all those years ago.

HELPING FOOT

Michels had one important bit of luck when establishing his legacy. When he was coach at Ajax, his best player was the Dutch forward Johan Cruyff. It was said that Cruyff was "four-footed", because he was the first player to kick with the outside as well as the inside of his foot. Cruyff understood Michels' ideas about "total football" better than anyone. He even pointed and told his teammates where to make runs during matches. Cruyff also played for Barcelona when Michels was coach there.

I'M on aLL fours!

When Cruyff stopped playing he also became a coach, first at Ajax and then at Barcelona, just like his former boss. At Ajax, Cruyff made sure that the team played in the Michels style. And they still do today – from the Under-11s right up to the senior team. At Barcelona, Cruyff did the same thing. Michels' philosophy became Cruyff's philosophy. Today the Barcelona youth academy, where Lionel Messi and many other great players were trained, still teaches its young stars to play in the way invented by Michels and continued by Cruyff. And it works.

WORLD PHILOSOPHY

In recent years, Barcelona have turned more players into coaches than any other team. Take Pep Guardiola, the Spanish midfielder, who played in the team for eleven years and went on to coach Barcelona to six trophies in a single year in 2009.

> Pep Guardiola was the most successful coach in Barcelona's history, winning three League titles and two Champions Leagues, as well as the Spanish Cup, the Spanish Super Cup, the UEFA Super Cup and the Club World Cup.

In fact, ten of Guardiola's teammates, some of whom were coached by Cruyff in 1996, became coaches at clubs all over the world. Michels' original philosophy is now a global phenomenon.

 ## MICHELS' PHILOSOPHY AROUND THE WORLD

BARCELONA 1996 PLAYER	TEAMS WENT ON TO COACH
Abelardo	Sporting Gijon
Guillermo Amor	Adelaide United
Sergi Barjuán	Almeria
Laurent Blanc	Bordeaux/France/PSG
Luis Enrique	Celta Vigo/Roma/Barcelona
Albert Ferrer	Real Mallorca

DUTCH DELIGHT

Another of Michels' legacies is the stunning success of Dutch football. The Netherlands, whose population is not even in the top ten in Europe, often do well at World Cups. Consider that England did not even reach a single final in the 48 years after winning the World Cup in 1966. Well, the Netherlands, four times smaller, have reached THREE finals and TWO semi-finals since then.

The Netherlands also produce more successful football coaches than other small countries. Over 50 years after Michels first took the job as Ajax coach, his methods are still being used. That's why some people call him the inventor of modern football. Cruyff carried on his work, but Michels was football's most important philosopher.

BARCELONA 1996 PLAYER	TEAMS WENT ON TO COACH
Óscar García	Mac. Tel Aviv/Brighton/RB Salzburg
Pep Guardiola	Barcelona/Bayern Munich/Man. City
Julen Lopetegui	Spain Under-21s/Porto
Juan Antonio Pizzi	San Lorenzo/Valencia/Chile
Robert Prosinečki	Red Star Belgrade/Azerbaijan
Hristo Stoichkov	Bulgaria/CSKA Sofia

RIDDLE ME THIS

Johan Cruyff was also regarded as being a football philosopher, often because of his enigmatic or puzzling remarks. Here are five of his classic lines:

Playing football is very simple, but playing simple football is the hardest.

There is only one ball, so you need to have it.

If I wanted you to understand it, I would have explained it better.

In my teams, the goalie is the first attacker, and the striker the first defender.

Before I make a mistake, I don't make that mistake.

TULIP FEAVER

STAR PUPIL

66 Don't stand there like a windmill! 99

STAR PUPIL Stats

Pairs of boots: 5
Pairs of clogs: 15
Number of feet plays with: 4
Daily intake of Edam: 1 kg
Birthplace: Orange County, USA
Supports: Barcelona (Spain)
Fave player: Johan Cruyff
Trick: Plays in any position

PHILOSOPHY QUIZ

1. Which philosopher came up with the line "Cogito, ergo sum"?

a) René Descartes
b) Plato
c) Dele Alli
d) Aristotle

2. The word "philosophy" comes from two Greek words: "philo", which means "lover of", and "sophia", which means what?

a) Wisdom
b) Laughing
c) Girls
d) Sofas

3. Which of the following coaches has NOT worked as a teacher?

a) Rinus Michels
b) Jose Mourinho
c) Pep Guardiola
d) Louis van Gaal

4. Complete the quote by French philosopher Albert Camus: "All that I know most surely about morality and obligation, I owe to..."

a) Tintin
b) Goalkeepers
c) Football
d) Antoine Griezmann

5. Which clever man said, "If you want to live a happy life, tie it to a goal, not to people or things"?

a) Albert Einstein
b) Petr Cech
c) Stephen Hawking
d) Jean-Paul Sartre

PHOTOGRAPHY

Taking photos of a football match is easy, right? Since all you do is point your camera at the pitch and press a button. Well, it's a little bit more complicated than that.

The job of a professional photographer at a match is a little bit like the job of a footballer: you need to have great technique, be fast, create chances and have a good intuition for the game. The thrill of getting a great picture is like the thrill of scoring a great goal. In this lesson you'll learn how to take a knockout photo. But first we need to understand just how a camera works. Smile!

LET THERE BE LIGHT

The eye is an amazing organ. When you see an object, light rays reflect off that object, pass through a **lens** at the front of your eye and register an **image** at the back of your eye. To start with this image is upside down. Our brains turn it the right way up – otherwise we would get very dizzy.

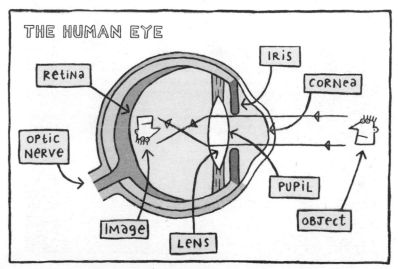

THE HUMAN EYE

Retina · Iris · Cornea · Optic Nerve · Pupil · Object · Image · Lens

A camera is a mechanical eye. The front part has a lens and the back part has a **sensor**, where the image is captured.

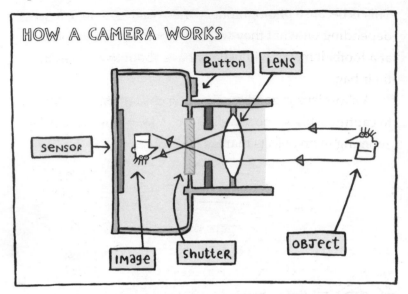

HOW A CAMERA WORKS

Button · LENS · SENSOR · IMage · Shutter · OBJect

The image on the back sensor is also upside down, and this time the computer in the camera turns it the right way up.

The camera also has a **shutter**, which is just in front of the back sensor. The shutter makes sure no light can get to the back. When you press the **button** on the camera it opens the shutter for a brief moment, letting the light reach the sensor and creating the photograph.

When taking pictures of footballers during a game, a photographer will set the shutter to open for only 1/1600 of a second per picture. If it is open for any longer, there is a risk the footballers will move and the picture will be blurred.

BAG OF LENSES

Professional cameras come in two parts: the **body** (which has the sensor, the button and the shutter) and the lens. This is because photographers often need to change lenses depending on what they want to shoot. A photographer at a football match will usually have about five lenses in their bag.

A short lens is good for shooting objects that are close, or to capture a big scene at a distance. A long lens is good for zooming in on objects that are far away.

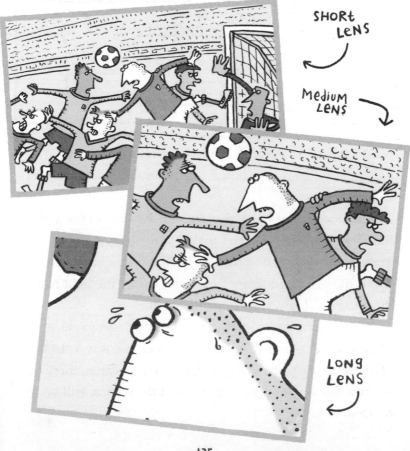

SHORT LENS

Medium LENS

LONG LENS

The biggest lenses are just like telescopes. They are so long and heavy that photographers have to balance them on a stick to take the weight.

MATCH ROUTINE

A photographer will arrive about three hours before kick-off to set up and get in position. They will be allocated a spot near the touchline where they must stay for the length of the match.

Once the starting whistle has blown, the photographer's job is to take pictures of the *significant* moments in a game.

What are these moments? Goals, definitely; important saves; perhaps crucial fouls or tackles. These are the shots that the newspapers and websites want to have.

Like a hunter tracking an animal through the viewfinder of a gun, most photographers will be tracking the ball through the viewfinder of their camera. Even the language of hunting and photography are similar: you *shoot* with a gun and you *shoot* with a camera.

Usually the action is where the ball is, so a photographer will always be watching it. But they will also have half an eye on the rest of the pitch, as football is very fast and unpredictable.

When the ball is near the goal the photographers will be tensing their fingers ready to take a picture – but not just one picture. A professional sports camera has a motor attached to the button, so when you press down it takes twelve pictures a second. Click-click-click-click-click-click-click-click-click-click-click-click. It's more like a machine-gun than a camera.

You need to take so many photos one after another because the action is so fast you may otherwise miss the moment when a player shoots.

If a match is exciting, a photographer may take more than a thousand pictures during it, which is about a picture every five seconds. If the match is boring, they may take a hundred or so, which is about one picture a minute.

Once a goal has been scored you don't need a picture of the ball in the net. All balls and all nets look the same. You want a picture of the scorer celebrating! The joyful expression on their face will tell the story.

An experienced photographer will also make sure they are aware of what is happening off the pitch. Sometimes the behaviour of the manager on the touchline or a group of colourful fans in the stadium can make for a brilliant photo that explains the game.

A good picture should not only capture the moment, but it must also be in **focus** and well **framed**.

FOCUSING

When you point a camera at an object in the distance the object will usually be blurred. The process of making the image sharp and clear is called **focusing** and involves a subtle adjustment of the lens.

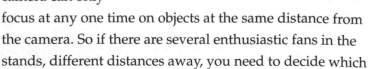

Thankfully all modern cameras have autofocus, which means that the focusing is done automatically by computer.

However, a camera can only focus at any one time on objects at the same distance from the camera. So if there are several enthusiastic fans in the stands, different distances away, you need to decide which one you want to have in focus. The photographer decides which part of the picture to have in focus using the viewfinder, which in Nikon cameras often looks like this.

There are 51! Count 'em!

The photographer has a choice of 51 parts of the image to focus on, each indicated by a little box. Using their thumb, they can move through the boxes to select the one they want.

YOU'VE BEEN FRAMED

To get a good picture you need to be fast with your eyes, fingers and thumbs. But it is not just about technique: a great photographer is also an artist.

If you are taking a picture of a footballer, ideally you want them in the centre of the image, or **frame**. What you don't want is the top of their head cut off or another player in the way, or something distracting in the background.

The best photographs are like paintings. The difference is that with a painting you can choose what you want to show. With a photograph you can only capture what happens in front of you.

In fact, taking great football pictures is a real challenge. There are a lot of things to remember: getting the right lens, making sure it is in focus, framing the shot – and not missing the moment. Rob MacNeice, senior camera expert at Nikon, told us that the speed and unpredictability of the game means that Premier League football is one of the most difficult sports to photograph in the world.

RACE TO PUBLISH

Many cameras are now set up with wireless transmitters that send pictures as soon as they are taken to a dongle in the photographer's pocket. From the dongle they are transmitted via satellite to the sports desk of a newspaper or website. The picture editor will then choose the best one to use. It can take as little as ten seconds for a picture to go from the camera to being available for everyone to see online.

STAR PUPIL

PAT PARAZZI

" Say cheese! "

STAR PUPIL Stats

Number of lenses in bag: 6
Photo albums at home: 356
Speed of light: 671 million mph
Birthplace: Panorama City, USA
Supports: Lens (France)
Fave player: Chris Kamara
Fave venue: Stadium of Light
Trick: Zooms around

PHOTOGRAPHY QUIZ

1. **Which of the following words also means photograph?**

   a) Snap
   b) Crackle
   c) Pop
   d) Fizz

2. **How many legs does a tripod have?**

   a) One
   b) Two
   c) Three
   d) Four

3. **After Arsenal won the FA Cup in 2015, midfielder Santi Cazorla was celebrating by the goal line when he picked up a camera that had been left there by a photographer. What did he do next?**

   a) He threw it into the crowd.
   b) He pretended it was a ball and kicked it into the air.
   c) He took a selfie of himself and his teammates.
   d) He ran off with it.

4. **A paparazzo is:**

   a) an Italian photographer who specializes in the Serie A football league.
   b) a photographer who takes shots of celebrities and their partners in public places and sells them to magazines and websites.
   c) an affectionate name for the eldest and most fatherly photographer at a football match.
   d) a photographer who takes aerial shots of football matches from a parachute.

5. **Digital images are made up of tiny dots called pixels. For most sports pictures in magazines, how many pixels will fit in a line one inch (2.54 cm) long like this?**

   a) 50
   b) 150
   c) 300
   d) 1000

1 inch

BUSINESS STUDIES

Professional footballers can be really rich. The top players at Manchester United and Real Madrid will earn more in a single week than doctors, farmers, teachers, scientists, the prime minister, estate agents, gardeners, cabbies, chefs, airline pilots, soldiers, personal trainers, dog walkers and astronauts earn in a whole year. Why is it that being a footballer is one of the highest-paid jobs in the world? In this lesson we are going to look at how the business of football works, and see how it has changed over the last few decades. It might be hard to imagine now, but once upon a time footballers earned not much at all.

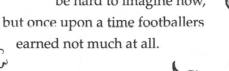

BUSINESS IS A PIECE OF CAKE

Let's start by looking at why footballers are so valuable. At the weekend we were at Football School's fête and there was only one slice left at the cake stand. We both love cake and were really hungry. Let's show you what happened.

The cake went to Ben, because he could afford to pay the most. And this is just what happens in football. Players are like slices of cake: clubs will pay as much as they have in their pockets for the slices of cake they want.

In other words, the best footballers are fantastically well-paid because their clubs can afford it. If you really want something you will pay as much as you can. So what we need to find out now is why clubs have so much money.

MONEY-GO-ROUND

Most businesses work on the basis that they will have money coming in (called **revenue**) and money going out (called **expenditure**).

MONEY OUT:

Players' wages.

Wages of other staff, such as the coach, the chef, the person who mows the pitch and the driver of the team bus.

Building the stadium and maintaining it once it is built.

MONEY IN:

Match tickets. Fans who want to see their team buy tickets for games and this money goes to the club.

TV rights. Broadcasters like Sky and BT Sport pay money to clubs for the right to show their games on their sports channels, because they know that fans will buy the subscriptions to watch those channels.

Sponsorship. Companies pay money to clubs to put their brand name on the front of the team's shirt or on the stadium, in order to get the brand seen by as many people as possible.

Merchandising. Fans buy official replica shirts, key rings, mugs, calendars and other licensed products, and some of this money goes back into the club.

Winning competitions. If you win the Premier League or the Champions League you get cash as well as a trophy.

Gifts. Some clubs have rich owners who will often dip their hands in their pockets to help out their team.

If you exclude gifts from owners and cash from trophies, all revenue ultimately comes from fans...

When we go to a match, we hand over money.

Ker-ching!

When we buy pyjamas with our team badge, we hand over money.

Ker-ching!

When we subscribe to a sports TV channel, we hand over money.

Ker-ching!

Football fans might not be rich, but there are millions of us. If we all pay small amounts through tickets, TV subscriptions and club shirts, then it soon adds up. Clubs have lots of money because of you and me. The money leaves our pockets and eventually arrives in footballers' pockets.

RICH GET RICHER

In business, if you have money already it is usually easier to make more money.

The richest clubs have the most money, so they can build the biggest stadiums. If they have the biggest stadiums, they can sell the most tickets. If they sell the most tickets, they make the most money. So they get even richer.

SUCCESS BREEDS SUCCESS

In football, if you have the best players already it is usually easier to carry on buying the best players.

The richest clubs can afford to buy the best players, so they have the best chance of winning trophies. The more trophies a club wins, the more prize money they get and the more TV money they get (because they will be shown on TV more often). So they will remain one of the richest clubs and will carry on being able to buy the best players.

MODERN MILLIONAIRES

You might assume that top footballers have always lived in mansions, driven expensive cars and worn snazzy clothes. But it's not true. The millionaire footballer is a recent phenomenon. Until 1961 footballers were only allowed to earn up to £20 a week, or about £400 a week in today's money, less than what a primary school teacher earns.

Footballers were so angry that they were paid so little, they threatened to stop playing unless they were allowed more money. The Football League caved in to the players' demands, and as soon as the £20 a week limit was lifted Johnny Haynes of Fulham became the best-paid player in the country, earning £100 a week (about £2,000 today).

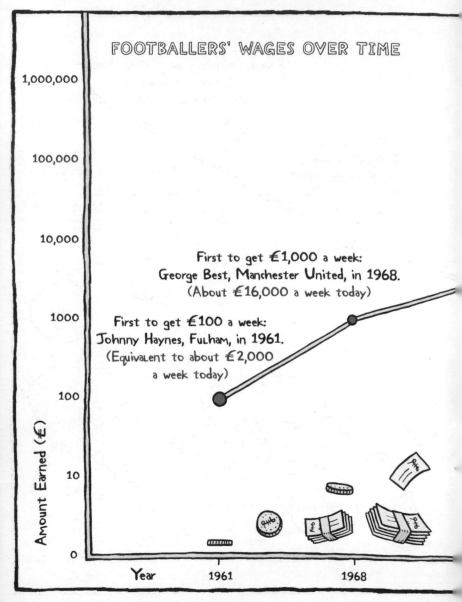

FOOTBALLERS' WAGES OVER TIME

First to get £1,000 a week:
George Best, Manchester United, in 1968.
(About £16,000 a week today)

First to get £100 a week:
Johnny Haynes, Fulham, in 1961.
(Equivalent to about £2,000
a week today)

Amount Earned (£)

Year   1961   1968

Here is a graph that shows the highest earning footballers of their day. The growth has been incredible: Ronaldo earns about 500 times what Haynes did in 1961.

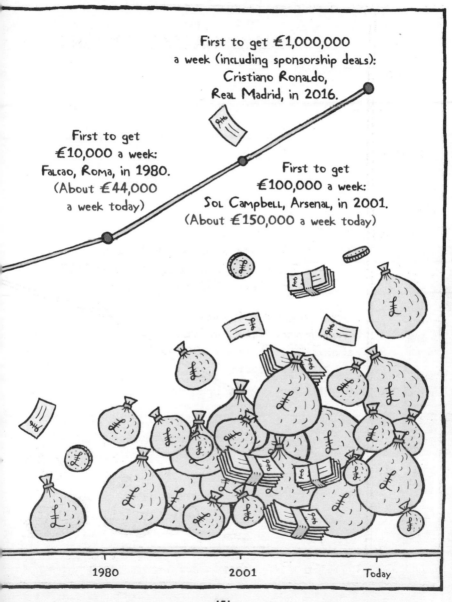

First to get €1,000,000 a week (including sponsorship deals): Cristiano Ronaldo, Real Madrid, in 2016.

First to get €10,000 a week: Falcao, Roma, in 1980. (About €44,000 a week today)

First to get €100,000 a week: Sol Campbell, Arsenal, in 2001. (About €150,000 a week today)

1980   2001   Today

Wages have risen so fast because there is now much more money in football. There are a few reasons for this:

1. Ticket prices have gone up and stadiums are bigger, so clubs make more money on match days.

2. The money paid to clubs for TV rights has increased  massively. TV companies can afford to pay clubs more, using the income from fans' subscriptions.

3. More football is shown on TV, with audiences watching all around the world. This has raised the profile of the game and clubs can now earn more money for sponsorship and merchandising deals.

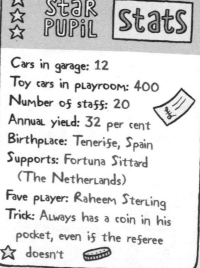

RICH LISZT

☆ STAR PUPIL

$

$

$

$

"Ker-ching!"

☆☆☆ STAR PUPIL

Stats

Cars in garage: 12
Toy cars in playroom: 400
Number of staff: 20
Annual yield: 32 per cent
Birthplace: Tenerife, Spain
Supports: Fortuna Sittard
(The Netherlands)
Fave player: Raheem Sterling
Trick: Always has a coin in his
pocket, even if the referee
☆ doesn't

BUSINESS STUDIES QUIZ

1. What is the currency in Spain?

a) The tortilla
b) The Spanish dollar
c) The peseta
d) The euro

2. If a footballer earns £1,000,000 in a week, how much do they earn per second?

a) 0.16p
b) 1.6p
c) 16p
d) £1.65

3. List the following from richest to poorest.

a) World's richest footballer
b) World's richest boxer
c) World's richest film star
d) World's richest banker

4. Manchester City is owned by Sheikh Mansour, one of the richest men in the world. Where is he from?

a) United Arab Emirates
b) Hong Kong
c) Egypt
d) Saudi Arabia

5. What did Cristiano Ronaldo, the highest-earning sportsman in the world, buy for his agent Jorge Mendes as a wedding present?

a) A copy of *Football School*
b) A pair of Mr and Mrs pillowcases
c) A Real Madrid season ticket
d) A Greek island

Thursday
Lesson 3+4

FASHION

The Blues! The Reds! The Whites! The Yellows!

No, we're not talking about Ben's collection of felt-tip pens, but about football clubs and their shirts. Shirt colour is such an important part of a club's identity that fans often use it as a nickname for the team. In this lesson we will learn how some famous clubs gained their distinctive colours.

And we'll look at national strips too. Why is it that some countries play in the colours of their national flag, but others don't? Behind every shirt there is a colourful story. But first we need to go back in time to the game's early days.

FOOTIE CAPS

In the middle of the nineteenth century, football teams didn't wear a standard kit. Instead players wore whatever they had. Sometimes that was cricket whites, since cricket was already an established sport by this time. In order to tell the teams apart, the players wore different coloured caps on their heads or sashes over their shirts.

But this could get confusing – imagine what would happen if everyone's caps fell off!

Excuse me sir, are you on my team?

Our new kit is bound to make headlines!

In the 1860s, the first English football clubs were founded. Over the next ten years, they decided that their players would wear coloured shirts. Many clubs took their team colours from schools – either ones where the founders had studied or ones with teams they admired. Blackburn Rovers, for example, based the half-and-half style of their kit on the strip of Malvern College, a school in Worcestershire.

COPY-KITS

Most early kits were colours such as white, black, blue or red because they were cheaper to buy. Clubs that were founded later on often based their strip on those of other more established teams.

TEAM	COLOURS	INSPIRED BY
Arsenal	red shirts	Nottingham Forest
Athletic Bilbao	red/white stripes	Southampton
Juventus	black/white stripes	Notts County
Leeds	white	Real Madrid

CROSBY TO CATALONIA

There's a story behind the colour of every team's kit. Look at the history of Barcelona's blue and red shirts. It's actually two stories, since no one knows which is correct.

Our first story begins in Crosby, near Liverpool, at the end of the nineteenth century. It's home to a famous school called Merchant Taylors'. The school's coat of arms has a lion on a blue background surrounded by red ornamental features. Note the colours: blue and red.

Sport-mad brothers Arthur and Ernest Witty went to school at Merchant Taylors'. After they left school they moved to Barcelona in Spain, where their dad ran a shipping company. Soon after October 1899 they became involved with a new football team called Barcelona. Their dad's company imported leather balls, nets and referee's whistles from England for the team to use.

Both Arthur and Ernest played for Barcelona and Arthur became the club president. And when the team had to decide on the colour of their strip they picked ... blue and red! It seems like the Witty brothers chose their old school colours for Barcelona.

The club was not well known at the time, but later became one of the most successful clubs in the world, winning La Liga and the Champions League many times. Barcelona's red and blue shirts are one of the most recognizable kits in sport, and they might have come from the colours of a school in the north of England.

But now for our second story. The other explanation for Barcelona's kit is that the Swiss founder of the club, who grew up in Basel in Switzerland, based it on Basel's colours – which are also blue and red.

Historians will debate the origins of this iconic kit until the end of time. But here at Football School we like to think that the real inspiration was Merchant Taylors'. We schools have got to stick together!

FOOTIE FRUITY

Barcelona are known as the Blaugrana, because of the red and blue colours of their kit. In Catalan, which is the language spoken in the city, "blau" means blue and "grana" comes from the word for "pomegranate", a reddish fruit. So "blaugrana" means "blue and pomegranate". Mmmm!

COLOUR BLIND

As we've just seen, kits are an important part of a club's identity. Fans can feel very protective of their team's colours. Just look at what happened to Cardiff City a few years ago.

In May 2010 Vincent Tan, a wealthy businessman from Malaysia, bought Cardiff City. Fans were very excited because he promised to spend lots of money to help the team get promoted to the Premier League.

But he had a condition: he wanted to change Cardiff's kit from blue to red. Now Cardiff City have worn blue since they first took that name in 1908. Not only that, but

they have a bluebird on their team badge and their nickname is the Bluebirds.

Tan had a proposal about that too. He wanted to change the bluebird to a dragon. And his reason for all of this? Tan said his lucky colour was red, which is associated with success in Asia.

Most fans protested, but Tan got his way. He spent about £70 million on the club and Cardiff City started playing in red. Some supporters were so angry they stopped going to games. But Tan's plan worked and Cardiff were promoted to the Premier League.

Then their fortunes changed again. They won only seven matches in the Premier League and finished bottom of the table.

Six months after relegation, Tan switched the kit back to blue and reinstated the bluebird on the team badge. He claimed his mother had reminded him of the importance of "togetherness, unity and happiness". The team might not have been winning as much, but at least the fans were happy again.

VISIONS OF BLUE

Cardiff City are known as the Bluebirds. Many other clubs are simply nicknamed the Blues:
And some national
teams too:

France
(Les Bleus)
Italy
(Azzurri)

Birmingham City
Chelsea
Everton
Ipswich Town
Shrewsbury Town
Southend United
Wycombe Wanderers

Come on you Blues!

WE'RE FLAGGING

But how do national teams decide what colours to wear? Most of them wear the colours of their country's flag.

This trend started with the first ever international game between England and Scotland in 1872. England wore white shirts to match the background colour of England's flag, which is called the St George's Cross. Scotland wore blue shirts to match the background colour of the Scottish flag, which is called the St Andrew's Cross.

England and Scotland still wear
these colours. England also usually
wear blue shorts, according to
the Football Association, historian
David Barber, because blue was the
FA's official colour. The three lions on the
England badge are blue for the same reason.
But who has ever seen a blue lion before?

OFF-COLOUR COUNTRIES

Some national kits don't reflect the colours of their flag at
all, which can be confusing.

The Netherlands' flag is red, white and blue, but
they wear orange. Italy's flag is red, white and green,
but they wear blue. Were their kit designers colour-blind?
Not quite...

Both strips make reference to old rulers. For the
Netherlands it is William of Orange, who led a Dutch
revolt against Spanish rule in 1568 that resulted in the
Netherlands' independence in 1648. Funnily enough, even
though William of Orange is a national hero, the town of
Orange that his name refers to is hundreds of
miles from the Netherlands in France. Even
funnier, this Orange has nothing to do
with the colour orange. It was named
Arausio after an ancient water god
by the ancient Romans, and over time
became the word "orange". Those
Dutch used a bit of artistic licence!

For Italy, their blue kit comes from one of the oldest royal families in the world, the Casa Savoia, who ruled from 1861 until 1946. Blue was their official colour, while their coat of arms, a white cross on red background, was the badge on Italy's kit at the 1934 World Cup. Here are some other countries whose kit doesn't match their flags:

TEAM	KIT	FLAG
Australia	green/gold	blue/white/red
Germany	white	black/red/yellow
India	blue	orange/white/green
Japan	blue	white/red
Slovenia	green/white	red/white/blue

ROY G. BIV

☆ STAR PUPIL

" Lighten up, man! "

☆
☆☆ STAR PUPIL   **STATS**
☆

Primary colours: 3
Main colours in rainbow: 7
Shirts in collection: 342
Crayons in desk: 25
Birthplace: Yellowstone National Park, USA
Supports: Suwon Samsung Bluewings (South Korea)
Fave player: Jamie Redknapp
Trick: Dazzling ball skills
☆

FASHION QUIZ

1. What fruit is associated with the kit colour of Barcelona?

a) Pineapple
b) Pomegranate
c) Raspberry
d) Clementine

2. Who lives in the White House?

a The Queen
b) The President of the USA
c) The England football team manager
d) Cristiano Ronaldo

3. What two colours do poetry experts say have no words to rhyme with them?

a) Turquoise and blue
b) Copper and sienna
c) Fuchsia and yellow
d) Orange and purple

4. Which Italian club produced a green and grey camouflage away strip in 2013?

a) Bologna
b) Perugia
c) Napoli
d) Torino

5. Which goalkeeper designed his own fluorescent kit to wear at the 1994 World Cup?

a) Jorge Campos (Mexico)
b) Claudio Taffarel (Brazil)
c) Bogdan Stelea (Romania)
d) Joseph-Antoine Bell (Cameroon)

COMPUTER SCIENCE

Being a top footballer is often really boring. You have lots of time with nothing to do. You spend hours on buses and planes to and from matches and hours in hotel rooms for away games or international tournaments. So it's not surprising that footballers like playing video games. Whenever we speak to players, they always tell us that it's their favourite way to relax and unwind. And even though they play real football almost every day, professional players also love to play football-based video games.

In this lesson we're going to learn about what computers are and how you can turn footballers, with all their individual skills, into video game characters.

We will also find out if playing video games can make you a better player. But you need to be careful – sometimes it can have a negative effect on your game. At Inter Milan, Swedish striker Zlatan Ibrahimović used to play video games for ten hours at a stretch. We suspect that it caused a drop in his performances. And when former England keeper David James let in three goals in one match, he blamed it on too much PlayStation. "I was getting carried away playing [it] for hours on end," he said.

NUMBERS GAME

A computer is an electronic machine that carries out tasks when you give it a **program**, or set of instructions. Computers store information using only the digits 0 and 1, which are called binary digits or **bits**. A group of eight bits is called a **byte**.

Video games are a type of program, which means they are made up of bytes. The information contained in the game *Football Manager* amounts to well over a **gigabyte**, which is a billion bytes. That's a lot of 0s and 1s.

In *Football Manager*, you are the coach of a club and you pick computer versions of real players for your team. Your team then plays against other teams. You decide which players to pick based on their individual strengths and characteristics.

What's exciting is that *Football Manager* is very realistic. Players perform just like they do in real life. To do this the game stores lots of information about each player as a set of numbers, which are then translated into bytes.

The numbers that define each player's characteristics are a mark out of 20. Players are scored on more than 250 qualities, such as:

ability, acceleration, adaptability, ambition, anticipation, concentration, corners, crossing, potential ability, decisions, dirtiness, dribbling, first touch, flair, free kicks, heading, injury proneness, jumping ability, leadership, loyalty, marking, natural fitness, passing, pressure, professionalism, stamina, strength, tackling, technique, teamwork, versatility, vision, work rate.

Once you start thinking about it, the list of qualities that make a good footballer is a very long one.

When your player faces an opponent during a match, the game has an **algorithm** – a step-by-step process – that decides what will happen next by comparing each player's numbers.

This system is exactly the same as that used by Match Attax cards. On a Match Attax card players are given marks for the following categories: Speed, Tackle, Power, Shoot, Skill, Pass, Defence and Attack. When you compare two players, the one who has the highest number in the relevant category wins.

Football Manager also compares players' numbers, but it does so in more than 250 categories, almost instantaneously, during every moment of the match. That's what makes it feel so realistic.

Alex	QUALITIES	Ben
10	Dress sense	15
20	Hairiness	7
6	Eating speed	19
12	Dance technique	12
19	Sense of humour	18
17	Fart power	4
1	Skill at spreading jam	20
5	Competence at walking dogs	20

QUALITY CONTROL

For *Football Manager* to be true to life, it needs to have the best data possible. The game has a network of 1,300 scouts, all around the world, who watch the real-life players closely so they can be as accurate as possible when they mark them out of 20 for the game.

If a player always wears the captain's armband and their teammates look up to them, they might score 20 on leadership. If they are so fat they can barely lift themselves off the ground, they might score a 1 on jumping ability.

But some qualities are more difficult to judge. How do you measure skill, ambition, heart or versatility? Or how much of an oddball they are?

Best Leap for headers

Most appearances as a sub

Leader

12

Football Manager gives goalkeepers a rating for eccentricity. It's a footballing cliché that goalkeepers are off their rockers. Many brilliant keepers have been notable characters, such as the Colombian René Higuita, who invented the scorpion kick, and the Liverpool hero Bruce Grobbelaar, who wobbled his legs to distract opponents during the 1984 European Cup final penalty shoot-out. Here are five cuckoo keepers.

NAME	COUNTRY	CRAZINESS
Fabien Barthez	France	Teammates would kiss his bald head before France games at 1998 World Cup
José Luis Chilavert	Paraguay	Scored free kicks and penalties when not defending his goal
Hugo Gatti	Argentina	Would pat strikers on the head after catching crosses
René Higuita	Colombia	Invented the scorpion kick, a clearance with the heels after a somersault
Jens Lehmann	Germany	Once appeared to wee behind the goal and borrowed a fan's glasses

cuckoo-est keeper

worst corner taker

FAMOUS FANS

When professional footballers play football video games, they are in the weird position of being able to pick computer versions of themselves for their teams.

French midfielder Paul Pogba was playing for Juventus when he appointed himself as manager of Chelsea on *Football Manager*. One signing he made was a French midfielder called … Paul Pogba. Was this an indication he wanted to move to Chelsea in real life? Pogba's *Football Manager* team was made public when the French Football Federation released footage of Pogba playing the game on its YouTube channel. It was actually a bit embarrassing for Pogba, because he'd dropped Chelsea's captain at the time, English defender John Terry, and picked only three of his Juventus teammates to play alongside him at Chelsea. Awkward!

Norwegian striker Ole Gunnar Solskjær, who once scored in the Champions League final for Manchester United, always wanted to become a coach. In preparation he played *Football Manager*, which he said taught him a lot about young players and management. When he finally did become a coach at Molde, his hometown club in Norway, he won the league in his first season.

TRAIN THE BRAIN

Video games are fun – but can they make you a better footballer?

The training staff at Manchester United thought so. They asked their footballers to play a game called *NeuroTracker*, where eight balls bounce around a screen. The aim is to follow four of the balls without getting distracted by the others. At the beginning of the session the player is told which four balls to follow, and at the end they are asked to point them out again. They get top marks if they get all four correct.

This game sounds pretty boring – there are no racing cars or battles or monsters – but it is thought that it improves concentration, focus and spatial awareness and sharpens reactions, all qualities that are required to be a good player.

Scientists are divided about whether "brain-training" video games like this one really can make you a better footballer. These games may well improve reaction times and motor skills – and will of course make you better at following four balls around a screen – but whether or not this is useful when playing in front of 90,000 fans at Wembley, no one yet knows. Even if Manchester United were hoping so!

RATINGS RELEGATION

A Premier League player once complained to the makers of a football video game because he felt his ratings in the game were unfairly low. He said that dressing-room morale was affected by it. But the video game company held firm and did not change his ratings. It was the right decision: the team finished bottom of the league and were relegated.

attributes	Rating
Tackling	2
Shooting	8
Teamwork	5
Moaning	98
Complaining	100

JOY STICK

★ STAR PUPIL

" Let's reboot! "

☆☆ STAR PUPIL Stats

Facebook friends: 121,395
Memory: 1 trillion gigabytes
Voltage: 24V
Hours playing Minecraft every day: 3.5
Birthplace: Ramsgate, England
Supports: Metalist Kharkiv (Ukraine)
Fave player: Mix Diskerud
Trick: Can freeze her position ☆

COMPUTER SCIENCE QUIZ

1. What is a megabyte?

a) A cool byte
b) A triple-decker sandwich
c) Something a shark does
d) A million bytes

2. Which of the following attributes are useful for a footballer?

a) Sense of smell
b) Musical taste
c) Loyalty
d) Likes animals

3. Which player spent three hours in the afternoon playing a football computer game before scoring in the World Cup final that night?

a) Ronaldo (Brazil, 2002)
b) Andrea Pirlo (Italy, 2006)
c) Andrés Iniesta (Spain, 2010)
d) Mario Götze (Germany, 2014)

4. Which team does the man who runs the *Football Manager* game support and has sponsored in the past?

a) Watford
b) Arsenal
c) Chelsea
d) West Ham

5. What was unique about the video game *FIFA 2016*?

a) You could change the hairstyles of players.
b) Players got injured during goal celebrations.
c) One tactical system you could play with used ten forwards.
d) It featured women's teams for the first time.

Football has an amazing capacity to bring people together.

Like when you make friends kicking a ball about in the park. Like when you meet someone who supports the same team as you and become friends for life. Like when the country goes football-crazy during the World Cup.

But football can also push people apart.

In this lesson we will see how the game can bring countries together and also create tensions between them. Because when two countries face each other, the match can be about more than just eleven players versus eleven players. It is about the collective hopes and fears of each nation.

Matters concerning how countries are run and how they get on with each other are what we call politics. Football can impact politics – sometimes for the good and sometimes for the bad.

CHRISTMAS TRUCE

The First World War lasted between 1914 and 1918 and involved the most powerful countries in the world at the time, with many others also joining in. Germany was on one side and the United Kingdom, France and Russia were on the other.

The main battlefield in Europe consisted of two lines of ditches, known as **trenches**, which ran alongside each other for hundreds of miles. British and French soldiers lived in the trenches on one side, and German soldiers lived in the trenches on the other side. Between the two lines was an area called **no man's land**, which was covered in barbed wire and sometimes only a few dozen metres wide. Soldiers who stepped onto no man's land would be immediately shot at by the enemy.

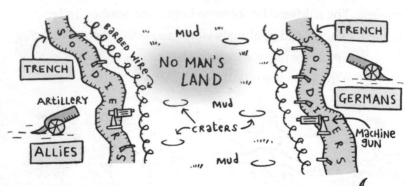

Life in the trenches was miserable and dangerous. It was dirty, cold, and infested by rats and constantly shaken by the thunder of guns and bombs. In December 1914, the German High Command sent Christmas trees to their trenches to cheer the soldiers up. A short distance away in the British trenches, the soldiers were also missing home and their families. When the Germans sang the Christmas carol "Silent Night" ("Stille Nacht" in German), one group of British soldiers heard them, applauded and asked for more.

On Christmas Day 1914 an incredible thing happened. In some of the trenches, British and German soldiers put down their weapons and walked into no man's land. But they didn't attack each other. Instead, they shook hands, exchanged gifts

and decided to play football together. The matches were chaotic. The soldiers' boots were heavy, the leather ball soon got soggy and goalposts were caps or helmets. Even more confusingly, some of the matches along the trenches were 100-a-side.

After the Christmas period the soldiers returned to their trenches and the war carried on as before. By the end of the war, the total number of soldiers who died was about eleven million. The Christmas Day truce of 1914 represented a moment of togetherness during one of the darkest times in European history. When they played each other at football, the British and the Germans were not enemies but friends.

SYMBOL OF PEACE

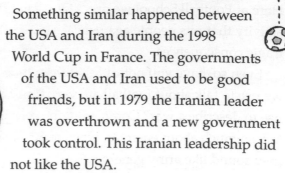

Something similar happened between the USA and Iran during the 1998 World Cup in France. The governments of the USA and Iran used to be good friends, but in 1979 the Iranian leader was overthrown and a new government took control. This Iranian leadership did not like the USA.

The two countries entered a period of hostility and distrust. They criticized each other a lot. When they were both drawn in the same group at the World Cup, organizers FIFA were worried that bad feelings and threats would overshadow the match.

Thankfully the game, which was played in France, passed peacefully. The Iran team gave each American player a bouquet of white roses, a symbol of peace in Iran, before kick-off. Iran won the game 2–1 but the impact went beyond the result. "We did more in 90 minutes than the politicians did in 20 years," said USA defender Jeff Agoos.

Things went so well, in fact, that the two countries played a friendly match against each other 18 months later in California. "[That] was far more significant because ... it needed the co-operation of both sides," said Mehrdad Masoudi, who worked with the Iran team at the World Cup fixture. "But it could only have happened if the match at France '98 was a success."

FIGHTING TALK

Here at Football School we don't like war. It is a nasty activity that pits people against each other with horrific and tragic consequences.

Even so, have you noticed that the words and phrases we use to talk about football are very similar to those we use to describe a war? Commentators, coaches and players talk so much about enemies, plans of attack and glory that they sound like army generals:

A player is deployed in an advanced role...

A player finishes from point-blank range...

A dropped player is a casualty...

The team is under fire...

The coach changes formation...

The clubs resume hostilities...

News from inside the camp...

Wingers provide ammunition...

The match is a battle...

SPORTING REGALIA

Another parallel between football and war is that both footballers and soldiers wear special clothes to do their jobs. Footballers wear kit and soldiers wear uniforms, and for much the same reasons, too:

ARMY UNIFORM	FOOTBALL KIT	PURPOSE
Chevrons on arm	Armband	To denote authority
Armour	Shin pads	For protection
Medals	Star for World Cup victory	To represent past honours
Insignia	Badge	To denote team/regiment

And there are other similarities between the world of a soldier and that of a footballer:

SOLDIER	FOOTBALLER	PURPOSE
Rosettes/scarves	Rosettes/scarves	To show allegiance
Flag	Fan banner	To show allegiance
General in control room	Coach in dugout	To give orders
Marching tune	Fans' chant	To improve morale
Animal on a standard	Three Lions	A mascot to defend

In international football the link between football and war is even more apparent. National teams stir up strong feelings and can rekindle historical resentments towards other countries. In one famous case, three World Cup qualifying matches served as a tipping point for a short but deadly war.

THE FOOTBALL WAR

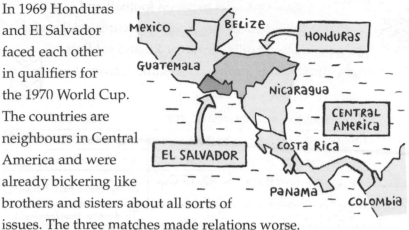

In 1969 Honduras and El Salvador faced each other in qualifiers for the 1970 World Cup. The countries are neighbours in Central America and were already bickering like brothers and sisters about all sorts of issues. The three matches made relations worse.

The first game was in Honduras. Newspapers reported that in order to stop the El Salvador team getting a good night's sleep, Honduran fans deliberately made lots of noise outside the team's hotel. After Honduras won 1–0, fans fought each other in the stadium.

The atmosphere was even more tense for the return game in El Salvador. The Salvadorans smashed the windows of the hotel where the Honduras team were staying and threw rotten eggs and dead rats through them. Fans had burned the Honduras flag, so when their national anthem was played a dirty dishcloth was run up the stadium flagpole instead. During the match, the pitch was lined with soldiers holding guns. Salvador won the game 3–0, causing riots of jubilation in the streets.

With one win each, there was to be a decider. Because of the escalating violence between the supporters of both teams, it was decided that the match would be played in another country – Mexico. The game was hard-fought and El Salvador scored in extra time to win 3–2.

Less than three weeks later the countries were at war. Salvadoran planes bombed Honduras and the Salvadoran army invaded. The war lasted four days (or 100 hours) and cost the lives of about 3,000 people, mostly civilians.

Even though the roots of the conflict were to do with things like jobs and migration and trade, the decision to go to war was a result of the fervent **patriotism** (love for your country) stoked up by the World Cup qualifiers. For that reason, the episode is now known as the Football War.

El Salvador didn't win a game, or score a goal, at the 1970 World Cup.

BATTLE FOR PEACE

But football can help bring about peace. It's the job of politicians to run countries – but sometimes they need a little bit of help. In Ivory Coast the striker Didier Drogba played an important role in ending a war between rival factions in his country. Drogba is Ivory Coast's most famous player. He was

GUINEA-BISSAU

MALi

BURKINA FASO

Guinea

ATLaNTiC OCEAN

SiERRA LEONE

YAMOUSSOUKRO

GHANA

LiBERiA

WEST AFRiCA

IVORY COAST

African Footballer of the Year twice and scored 104 goals for Chelsea.

In 2002 a **civil war** in Ivory Coast had been going on for five years. A civil war means that people in the same country are fighting each other, and in Ivory Coast hundreds, if not thousands had died. But also in 2005 the country qualified to play in the World Cup for the first time.

Ivory Coast's final qualifying match for the 2016 World Cup saw them win against Sudan. As soon as the full-time whistle blew, the players, who were all from different parts of Ivory Coast, celebrated with each other, hugging and dancing.

In the dressing-room afterwards, Drogba gave a live TV interview. "Men and women of Ivory Coast, from the north, south, centre, and west," he said. "We proved today that all Ivorians can co-exist and play together with a shared aim, to qualify for the World Cup. We promised you that the celebration would unite the people."

The players all went down on their knees. Drogba, from the south, was embraced by his teammate, Kolo Touré, from the north. "Pardonnez!" Drogba said. It means "forgive" in French. "Pardonnez! Pardonnez! Please lay down your weapons. Hold elections. All will be better."

His words helped bring the whole country together and made the warring factions listen to each other. It was reported that Drogba then spent months behind the scenes persuading the two sides to talk.

"Drogba [was] involved in lots of quiet, but successful, football diplomacy," said a report about football's role in bringing peace to Africa. "He personally intervened to convince [the opposing sides] to agree [to a peace treaty]."

Drogba said later, "I have won many trophies in my time, but nothing will ever top helping win the battle for peace in my country."

POLLY TICKS

STAR PUPIL

66 Let's vote on it! 99

☆☆☆ STAR PUPIL Stats

International relations: 8
Flags in collection: 136
Votes: 12 million
Length of term: 4 years
Birthplace: Westminster, England
Supports: New England Revolution (USA)
Fave player: Whoever is captain
Trick: Negotiating with the referee

POLITICS QUIZ

1. On what special day in 1914 did German and British soldiers lay down weapons and play football with each other?

a) New Year's Day

b) Easter Sunday

c) Christmas Day

d) Alex's birthday

2. What military term do coaches often shout at strikers?

a) Stand to attention

b) Take cover

c) Shoot

d) Form a phalanx

3. In which country did the boss of the biggest football club become president?

a) Argentina

b) Germany

c) Russia

d) USA

4. Which team does Prince William, who is President of the English FA, support?

a) Aston Villa

b) Crystal Palace

c) Queens Park Rangers

d) Newcastle United

5. Argentinian forward Diego Maradona claimed his goal against England in the 1986 World Cup was divine "revenge" for the Falklands War. But what did "God" use to score?

a) The Head of God

b) The Foot of God

c) The Hand of God

d) The Backheel of God

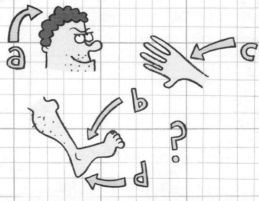

MUSIC

'Ere we go, 'ere we go, 'ere we gooooo!

Doesn't a singalong make the world seem a better place? It certainly makes football more fun to watch.

Football songs – or chants – are as old as the game itself. Singing brings the fans and the team together. Fans feel part of something bigger than themselves, and the team feel the support. Coaches sometimes say that the loud singing of fans plays a part in a victory. After all, players are just like everyone else, and respond better to cheers than boos. Imagine if *you* were playing football and someone booed every time you touched the ball. It would be hard to concentrate.

In this lesson, we will find out where football chants come from and why we sing them. We'll see how in some ways they are similar to ancient Greek poetry – although luckily we don't have to sing them in Greek.

We will also look at national anthems, which are sung before every international match played between two different countries. National anthems often reflect the personality of a whole country, and fans love to sing them as loudly as possible. Sometimes the players join in and sometimes they don't. At Football School we want everyone to sing along, whatever the tune – this lesson is going to be a noisy one!

FOOTBALL FOLK

Thousands of football songs have been written over the years and singing at games has become the norm. But there is no committee that meets during a match and decides what songs will be sung. There is no elected songwriter who writes or sings the funniest tunes of the day. Instead, anyone who has a song they want to sing simply stands up and sings it. If other people like it, they join in.

Some people see these songs as a form of **folk music**. The former Poet Laureate Andrew Motion, who was appointed by the Queen to write poetry for significant events (he wrote about important subjects such as war, bullying and climate change), described football chants as "a huge reservoir of folk poetry".

Folk music usually has no known composer and is passed from person to person by listening and repeating. This method of sharing was how some of the world's first poems came to be heard. The "Iliad" and the "Odyssey", which are believed to have been composed by the ancient Greek poet Homer, date back nearly 3,000 years. These epic poems weren't originally written down, but were passed from person to person by word of mouth, much like some of the most memorable football songs.

STAND UP... IF YOU LOVE HOMER...!

STEADY ON

The oldest football song that can still be heard in the stands today was written in the 1890s for a local factory team on England's east coast. It became the official song of nearby Norwich City when the team was founded in 1902. Today, over 100 years later, Norwich fans still sing it before every match.

On the Ball, City
Kick it off,
Throw it in,
Have a little scrimmage,
Keep it low,
A splendid rush,
Bravo, win or die;
On the ball, City,
Never mind the danger,
Steady on,
Now's your chance,
Hurrah! We've scored a goal.
City, City, City.

Rousing stuff or what!

The word "scrimmage" means struggle. It is used in different sports, most famously in rugby, where it gave us the word "scrum". It can also mean a practice match.

WHAT A TUNE

Football brings people together. If you are singing the same song as thousands of other fans, you feel close to them even if you don't know them. Celebrating your support for a team, even if they are losing, can be a joyful experience. The tunes of the songs are often well-known melodies or borrowed from recent pop songs.

CHANT ORIGINS

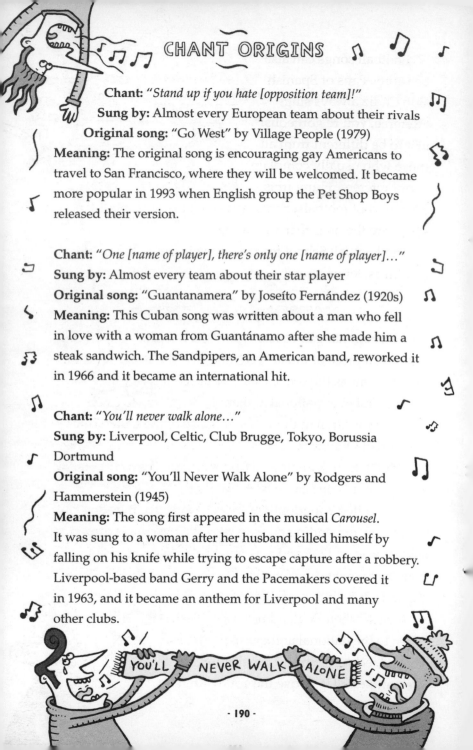

Chant: *"Stand up if you hate [opposition team]!"*
Sung by: Almost every European team about their rivals
Original song: "Go West" by Village People (1979)
Meaning: The original song is encouraging gay Americans to travel to San Francisco, where they will be welcomed. It became more popular in 1993 when English group the Pet Shop Boys released their version.

Chant: *"One [name of player], there's only one [name of player]…"*
Sung by: Almost every team about their star player
Original song: "Guantanamera" by Joseíto Fernández (1920s)
Meaning: This Cuban song was written about a man who fell in love with a woman from Guantánamo after she made him a steak sandwich. The Sandpipers, an American band, reworked it in 1966 and it became an international hit.

Chant: *"You'll never walk alone…"*
Sung by: Liverpool, Celtic, Club Brugge, Tokyo, Borussia Dortmund
Original song: "You'll Never Walk Alone" by Rodgers and Hammerstein (1945)
Meaning: The song first appeared in the musical *Carousel*. It was sung to a woman after her husband killed himself by falling on his knife while trying to escape capture after a robbery. Liverpool-based band Gerry and the Pacemakers covered it in 1963, and it became an anthem for Liverpool and many other clubs.

Football songs can also be funny. Fans of Spanish side Cádiz always sing, "Referee, you're gorgeous!" just to be different from all those who usually complain about referees. Humour is

JIMMY is great at conducting the Midfield.

a big part of football chants, and often the most popular songs are the ones that are funniest.

The Football School team also need a song. If you have any ideas, let us know!

NATIONAL ANTHEMS

At international games teams sing their country's **national anthem**, a piece of music recognized by the people and the government as the official song of the country.

The first ever national anthem took a while to catch on. It was written in the 1560s in praise of the Dutch ruler William of Orange, and was called "Het Wilhelmus" ("The William"). It took another 200 years before the next anthem emerged. This one came from England.

The United Kingdom's anthem, "God Save the King" (or Queen, depending on who is on the throne), became widespread in 1745 and was so popular that dozens of countries – including Sweden, Germany and Russia – used the same tune but sang different words.

In fact, when England next play Liechtenstein, listen to the national anthems before the game. Liechtenstein still use the tune for their anthem "Up above the Young Rhine".

Most anthems only became official in the 1920s. Nowadays, anthems divide into roughly five types:

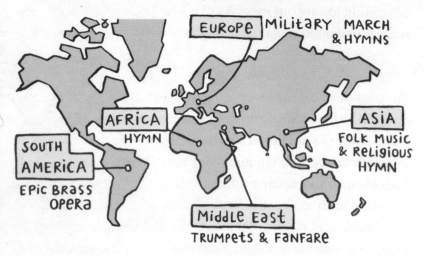

EUROPE MILITARY MARCH & HYMNS

ASIA FOLK MUSIC & RELIGIOUS HYMN

AFRICA HYMN

SOUTH AMERICA EPIC BRASS OPERA

Middle East TRUMPETS & FANFARE

Most fans love to sing the national anthem before an international match, but not all players do. Sometimes they stay silent, preferring to save their energy and focus on the game. Some have no option: Spain's national anthem has no words. The anthems of Uruguay and Argentina have long musical sections before the words begin, but because FIFA only allows 90 seconds for each anthem, the players often sing the words to the wrong tune.

Players have been criticized for not singing their national anthem. Some people think it means that they don't care about their country. Germany's team at the 2010 World Cup came under fire for not singing their national anthem, and the England coach at the time, Roy Hodgson, told his players they had to join in with "God Save the Queen" before matches at the 2014 World Cup. However his assistant coach Gary Neville never sang it before any of his 85 England games, as he said he was "focusing on the match". Singing didn't help England in 2014: they may have sung loudly but they didn't win a single match and went home bottom of their group.

♫ ♪ NATIONAL EMOTION

Love for your country is called **patriotism** and a national anthem plays an important part in this. Some countries are newer than others and their anthems can be very emotional for fans. When Yugoslavia broke up into different states in 1991, countries such as Croatia, Slovenia, Macedonia and Bosnia and Herzegovina were formed with their own national anthems. The Bosnia and Herzegovina anthem has caused some problems: politicians in the country have still not been able to agree on the best lyrics to keep everyone happy, so it has no words at all. In some countries where there has been conflict, such as Rwanda and Iraq, anthems have been used to try to heal divisions.

Fans of newer countries tend to display their patriotism more and sing their anthems loud and proud. That's because when a country is newer, the people who live there tend to love it a bit more and want to show it off – like Ben does when he wears brand new trainers.

Whatever team you're following, we recommend that you support them by singing loud and proud. The players will like it, and you will enjoy it too – even if your voice sounds like your granny screaming after she's stubbed her toe!

ALEX AND BEN'S SONGBOOK
TOP FIVE FAVOURITE NATIONAL ANTHEMS

BY NAME:

1. Senegal – "Pluck your Koras, Strike your Bafalons"
2. Norway – "Yes, We Love this Country"
3. Bangladesh – "My Golden Bengal"
4. Honduras – "Your Flag is a Heavenly Light"
5. Nepal – "Made of Hundreds of Flowers"

BY TUNE:

1. Italy – "The Song of the Italians"
2. Brazil – "Brazilian National Anthem"
3. France – "La Marseillaise"
4. Uruguay – "National Hymn"
5. USA – "Star-Spangled Banner"

CHANTELLE RHYMES

STAR PUPIL

"Higher!"

STAR PUPIL STATS

Whispers before she sings: "1-2-3-4"

Vocal range: 9 octaves

Top volume: 100 decibels

Beats per minute: 120

Birthplace: Singapore

Supports: Seattle Sounders (USA)

Fave player: Alex Song

Trick: A master of the one-two

MUSIC QUIZ

1. **The Netherlands has the world's oldest national anthem. It is called:**

a) Boring Tune
b) The Bit We Hum
c) Tra-La-La-La-Boom-Di-Ay
d) The William

2. **Which of the following is a line from the Real Madrid anthem "Hala Madrid"?**

a) "I wear your shirt right next to my heart!"
b) "We are called Real Madrid because we are real!"
c) "Madrid has the best restaurants in the world!"
d) "We love you more than we love life!"

3. **Which is the only country in the world to have a national anthem that was co-written by its president?**

a) Kazakhstan
b) Bolivia
c) North Korea
d) Swaziland

4. **Finish the classic song title by 1990s pop group Half Man Half Biscuit: "All I want for Christmas is a..."**

a) Racing Genk home kit
b) Admira Wacker home kit
c) Dukla Prague away kit
d) Skonto Riga away kit

5. **What lyrics did Portuguese club Porto complain to UEFA about, after Manchester City fans made up a tune about their Brazilian forward Hulk?**

a) "You're not incredible!"
b) "You're green and you know you are!"
c) "Stand up if you smell Hulk!"
d) "Where is your Spiderman?"

PHYSICS

I **love** physics! Alex, are you all right?

I feel a bit spaced out.

Sing a song about a planet, that will sort you out.

You mean, a Nep-tune?

The atmosphere in this class will be great. You all set?

Just one question: what would you do if you saw a spaceman?

Park in it, man!

L et's start our final lesson of the week with some bad news: we're all doomed!

The number of people on Earth is growing, and we are running out of space for homes and growing food. There will come a time when there is no room left.

Now for the good news: there's a whole universe out there to explore.

We're going to leave Football School far behind and see if it is possible to play football on Mars.

NepTuNe

URaNUS

SaTURN

THE SOLAR
SYSTEM
(NOT TO SCALE)

AsTeRoid BelT

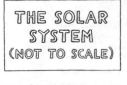

JUPiTeR

EaRTh MaRS

VeNUS

MeRcURY

The
SUN

Mars is the planet next to Earth in our solar system and the one scientists think is most suitable for human colonization.

Are you ready to visit the red planet? Five. Four. Three. Two. One. BLAST OFF!!!

COLD AND DARK

There are many challenges to living on Mars. Firstly, it is bum-spankingly cold. The average temperature is about –60°C, the same as winter in the South Pole. Secondly, there's not enough oxygen in the atmosphere. Humans need oxygen in order to breathe, so if we went outside we would need to wear oxygen masks at all times.

Thirdly, there is about half the amount of light as there is on Earth, since it is further from the sun.

Still, these are only minor inconveniences and they would not stop us from playing football – if not outside, then on floodlit indoor pitches.

WHAT AN ATMOSPHERE

However, football on Mars would be a very different game from the one we enjoy on Earth. This is because of phenomena that it's impossible to do anything about.

When you kick a ball on Mars it will go much higher and travel much further than when you kick one on Earth. This is for two reasons:

1. GRAVITY

The force that makes objects fall to the ground when you drop them is called **gravity**. The gravity on Mars is about a third of the gravity on Earth. This is mainly because Mars is a smaller and lighter planet than Earth.

If you drop a ball on Mars it will fall to the ground more slowly than it would if you dropped it on Earth. So when you kick a ball on Mars, it will travel much further before it lands than on Earth, as it is not being pulled down as quickly.

If you kick a ball upwards on Mars it will go much higher, too. When a goalkeeper takes a goal kick, they will easily shoot the ball out of the stadium.

The lower gravity will also mean that you can jump about three times higher than you could on Earth. This will make headers a lot more entertaining.

2. AIR RESISTANCE

Air is what we call the invisible gases that surround the earth. These gases – mostly nitrogen and oxygen – are made up of tiny **particles**. But what are particles? Wave your hand quickly in front of you and you will feel a gust. That's the feeling of billions of particles hitting your hand. When a football moves through air, it will also cause a gust. The air particles that are in the way of the ball slow it down. This effect is called **air resistance**.

There is also air on Mars – mostly a gas called carbon dioxide – but it is about a hundred times thinner than the air on Earth. In other words, the air on Mars has far fewer particles in it. A kicked ball will travel further because there are fewer gas particles slowing it down.

☆ DON'T BEND IT LIKE...

The tiny amount of air resistance on Mars means that playing football will be different in another way, too: it will be impossible to bend the ball when you kick it. On Earth, in order to curve a free kick or a corner you need to slice the ball, so that it spins as it moves. The spinning ball hits the air particles and this causes it to curve. But if you slice a ball on Mars, the spinning ball will not curve because there are not enough particles for it to hit.

Players who are famous for curling their free kicks would be rubbish on Mars.

FAMOUS
FREE-KICK TAKERS
David Beckham (England)
Ronald Koeman (The Netherlands)
Siniša Mihajlović (Serbia)
Juninho Pernambucano (Brazil)
Andrea Pirlo (Italy)

FUTURE FOOTBALL

So playing football on Mars will be a challenge. A future FMFA (Fédération Martien de Football Association) will have to decide whether to counter the problems by changing the rules of the game.

In order to make sure the ball does not travel such long distances, players will have to learn to kick it with less force than normal. Or the FMFA could introduce a much heavier, less bouncy ball. But these options might make matches slow and boring to watch.

Another option for the FMFA would be to increase the size of the pitch so that players could kick the ball further, but this might make it unpleasant for fans, who may need to bring binoculars to see what is going on.

Football can make the transition to Mars – but only time will tell if the Martians are going to enjoy it quite as much as we do now.

ANOTHER PLANET

Planets in the solar system that are more distant than Mars present even bigger challenges for football.

PLANET	MAIN PROBLEM	OUTCOME
Venus	460 °C	Ball melts
Jupiter	No solid surface	Running on liquid
Neptune	Too windy	Ball flies away

VENUS SUPERNOVA

☆ Star Pupil

" Cosmic! "

☆☆☆ Star Pupil Stats

Average jump: 3 metres
Thickness of football jersey: 5 centimetres
Daily commute from Mars: 8 months
Sock fluorescence: 500 units
Birthplace: Rock, England
Supports: LA Galaxy (USA)
Fave surface: Astroturf
Trick: Hanging in the air
☆

PHYSICS QUIZ

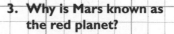

1. Which planet is closest to the sun?

a) Saturn
b) Mercury
c) Venus
d) Jupiter

2. What does gravity explain?

a) Why this book falls to the floor when you drop it
b) Why iron nails stick to a magnet
c) Why you can't breathe on Mars
d) Why gravy is delicious

3. Why is Mars known as the red planet?

a) The person who discovered it supported Manchester United.
b) It is very hot.
c) It is covered with red dust.
d) It used to be called RedLand.

4. Which American team did English midfielder David Beckham play for?

a) New York Cosmos
b) Houston Dynamo
c) LA Galaxy
d) Colorado Comets

5. Which recently discovered galaxy was named after a footballer?

a) Red Star 7, named after Raheem Sterling
b) Cosmos Redshift 7, named after Cristiano Ronaldo
c) Luminous Meteor 9, named after Lionel Messi
d) Novo Golaço 9, named after Neymar

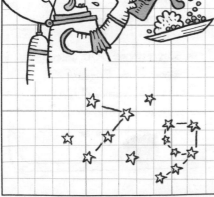

QUIZ ANSWERS

BIOLOGY
1. d
2. b
3. b
4. c
5. d

ENGLISH
1. c
2. d
3. b
4. c
5. c

MATHS
1. a
2. c
3. c
4. a
5. b

ZOOLOGY
1. c
2. a
3. c, dragon
4. a
5. b

PHSE
1. b
2. a
3. a
4. c
5. b

HISTORY
1. b
2. c
3. c
4. a
5. a

PSYCHOLOGY
1. b
2. b
3. b
4. c
5. b

DESIGN TECHNOLOGY
1. c
2. d
3. b
4. a
5. c

GEOGRAPHY
1. b
2. a
3. d
4. c
5. d

DRAMA
1. a
2. a
3. b
4. c
5. a

PHILOSOPHY
1. a
2. a
3. c
4. c
5. a

PHOTOGRAPHY
1. a
2. c
3. c
4. b
5. c

BUSINESS STUDIES
1. d
2. b
3. d c a b
4. a
5. d

FASHION
1. b
2. b
3. d
4. c
5. a

COMPUTER SCIENCE
1. d
2. c
3. b
4. a
5. d

POLITICS
1. c
2. c
3. a
4. a
5. c

MUSIC
1. d
2. a
3. a
4. c
5. a

PHYSICS
1. b
2. a
3. c
4. c
5. b

ACKNOWLEDGEMENTS

All the best teams need support from other people. Alex and Ben were thrilled to have illustrator Spike Gerrell as their teammate. Spike, you are a genius.

We were lucky that friends, family and experts were happy to contribute to Football School in many different ways. Our agents Rebecca Carter and David Luxton always offered the right advice and encouragement.

We couldn't have wished for a more enthusiastic, dedicated and creative squad at Walker Books. There's only one Denise Johnstone-Burt, Daisy Jellicoe, Iree Pugh, Louise Jackson and Alice Primmer!

We would like to thank the following for their time and expertise:
Peter Alegi, Alan Ames, Tim Angel, David Barber, Rosa Bransky,
Ciaran Brennan, Razvan Burleanu, Greg Cohen, Pete Etchells,
Dion Fanning, Ian Forgacs, Tai Foster, James Hartnett, Eagle Heights,
Stephen Hunt, Leigh Ireland, Miles Jacobson, Professor David James,
Tom Jenkins, Simon Kuper, Andrew Lawn, Steve Lawrence,
Mark Lyttleton, Robert MacNeice, Alex Marshall, Steve McNally,
Don McPherson, Mark Miodownik, James Montague, Ben Oakley,
Sarah Oakley, Sam Pilger, Josh Rattet, Adam Rutherford, Richard Sadlier,
David Spiegelhalter, Alan Spurgeon, Luis Vidigal, David Winner.

Thanks to our original Star Pupils: Dylan Auerbach, Joe Baden-Powell, Rafi and Zak Bartfeld, Maya and Joshie Greenslade, Thibaut Lyttleton, and Saul and Gabriel Pardon.

Alex would like to thank Ruth Shurman and Roman Pardon for helping with the germination of the idea. He couldn't have done it without Natalie's love and encouragement and Zak's early morning wake-up calls.

Ben would also like to thank Annie for her inspiration and support; and Clemmy and Bibi, the sweetest proof-readers anyone could wish for.

ABOUT YOUR COACHES

Alex Bellos writes about maths for the *Guardian* and is the author of two works of popular science, *Alex's Adventures in Numberland* and *Alex Through the Looking-Glass* as well as the mathematical colouring book *Snowflake Seashell Star*. He has also written *Futebol: The Brazilian Way of Life*, which was shortlisted for Sports Book of the Year, and he ghost-wrote Pelé's bestselling autobiography.

Ben Lyttleton is a journalist, broadcaster and football consultant. He is the author of *Twelve Yards: The Art and Psychology of the Perfect Penalty* and his football articles have been published in over 20 countries. He is a director of Soccernomics, a football consultancy that helps teams improve their performance.

AND YOUR ILLUSTRATOR

Spike Gerrell grew up loving both playing football and drawing pictures. As an illustrator, he now gets to draw pictures for a living. At heart though, he will also always be a central midfielder.